DEC 06 1995			
NOV 0 7 1998			
JAN 0 3 2005			
FEB 0 7 2005			
DEC 1 4 2006			
261-2500		Printed in USA	

THE ENTREPRENEUR AS CEO
Building a Business

By Donn D. Dears

WDD Publishing, Plano Texas

THE ENTREPRENEUR AS CEO
Building a Business

By Donn D. Dears

Published by:
WDD Corporation
4757 West Park Blvd.
Suite 106-124
Plano, TX 75093

Publisher's Cataloging in Publication Data.
Dears, Donn D.
The Entrepreneur as CEO: Building a Business/ by Donn D. Dears.
Includes index.
1. Success in Business.
2. Entrepreneurship.
3. New Business Enterprises.
4. Small Business.
5. Management.
658.4 DDC20 91-91038
ISBN 0-9629752-1-4 : $22.95 Hardcover
ISBN 0-9629752-2-2 : $10.95 Softcover.

Table of Contents

TOPIC HEADINGS

Dedicated to my son and daughter, Bill and Elizabeth.
Written so they can benefit from my experience.
Also dedicated to my wife Marion who tolerated endless
weekends of work and years of travel.

Preface

Few activities are as rewarding as building a business. If this is your objective, I want to help. It is taken for granted that you have the motivation, energy and vision to succeed. Let me provide some of the experience.

The Entrepreneur as CEO deals with issues that are critical to success during each stage of a company's development. The book has four parts, each devoted to one of the four stages of a company's life cycle. They are.

1. The seed and start-up stage.

2. The takeoff stage.

3. The growth stage.

4. Beyond the growth stage.

Each part is sub-divided into five sections dealing with the critical issues affecting the CEO's five key responsibility areas. The CEO's five key responsibility areas are:

1. Cash.

2. Strategy.

3. Marketing.

4. Operations.

5. People.

Actions required of the CEO are spelled out in each section. From raising money to pricing for market share the entrepreneur needs sound judgement. And of course good luck.

Warning & Disclaimer

This book is designed to provide perspective on many situations that confront an entrepreneur starting a new business. Business situations vary and it is the responsibility of the reader to use good judgement when applying the suggestions contained in this book.

This book is sold with the understanding that the author and publisher are not engaged in rendering legal or accounting services. If legal or accounting assistance is required, the services of a competent lawyer or CPA should be sought.

The author and WDD Corporation shall have neither liability nor responsibility to any person or entity with respect to any loss or damage caused, or alleged to be caused, directly or indirectly by the information contained in this book.

If you do not wish to be bound by the above, you may return this book with the purchase receipt to the publisher for a full refund of your purchase price.

What is required to survive? To succeed?

Most entrepreneurs want to get rich. Many want fame. Survival, success, and acclaim are stages in the career of a great CEO.

Entrepreneurs who will be the CEO's of their new companies, expect to succeed. Sadly, many will fail. Only a few will become wealthy. Fewer still will become legends.

The statistics are discouraging. Only one in ten companies in which venture capitalists invest are enormously successful. Two are absolute failures. The remaining seven muddle along, with half of them derisively referred to as the walking dead.

What is required for a CEO to survive? To succeed? To be great? How can the entrepreneur beat the odds and become rich? A vision for the enterprise is essential; as are determination, intelligence and hard work. But to be successful requires mastering the fundamentals.

Some CEO's have had great teachers and learned the fundamentals as their careers progressed. Other CEO's, thrown into their position, are quick enough and lucky enough to survive. "The Entrepreneur as CEO" is intended to help those who haven't been lucky enough to have had a great teacher. Or won't be lucky enough to have sufficient time to learn on the job. There is another aspect about fundamentals that is a curious phenomenon. Managers assume that once mastered, the fundamentals will always be followed. During the seventies I had responsibility, with other General Managers, for a very successful worldwide decentralized business, approaching a billion dollars in sales. The business had many geographically dispersed profit and loss centers, with considerable autonomy delegated to local management. Many mistakes made by local managers were the same mistakes that others had previously made. Either we hadn't communicated our experience to the newer managers or we, and they, had ignored the warning signs that should have alerted everyone.

Even experienced CEO's fall into the trap of assuming the organization has learned from its past mistakes. The "organization" may know better, but people change positions and the new person may not have had the same experience as the previous manager. People also forget; and people tend to be optimistic about the outcome of a problem.

One trait the CEO must develop to survive is constant awareness. This requires active participation, open communications and involvement. The corner office cannot become a bastion, shielding and protecting its occupant from criticism and reality. The world is changing too rapidly.

The life cycle of a company.

Every product has a life cycle curve and every company initially follows the curve of its first product. Most companies begin by offering a single, or very narrow, product line or service. When the initial offering becomes a success and reaches the knee of its growth curve, management begins to explore how it can extend the company's life cycle.

The life cycle of a new company can be divided into four stages as depicted in Figure 1. They are:

1. The seed and start-up stage.

2. The takeoff stage.

3. The growth stage.

4. The maturing stage.

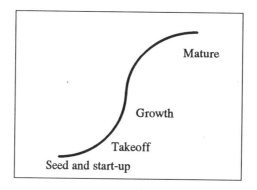

Figure 1

The actions required of the CEO are distinctly different during each of these stages.

A generation ago a product's life cycle extended over twenty years. Today, a better estimate for the average product life cycle is ten years. Some high technology products have life cycles of only three years. This means that unless there is corporate renewal, today's successful start-up will be someone else's cash cow ten years from now.

The length of each stage will vary between companies. The seed and start-up stage can last for ten or more years, but is usually much shorter. The typical duration of each stage is shown below.

1. Seed & start-up	1 to 3 years.
2. Takeoff	1 to 2 years.
3. Growth	3 to 8 years.
4. Maturing	Continuing.

The maturing company either continues to regenerate itself or enters a period of decline.

This rough timetable provides a framework for structuring the work that must be completed during each stage of the company's growth, if the company is to reach its full potential. Each company should judge the appropriateness of these time frames for its product or service.

Some exceptional companies will move through the early stages at lightning speed. If they are to survive, these companies must do the critical organizational work in a time frame compressed to the point of absurdity. Compaq Computer and Sun Microsystems are examples of exceptional companies.

Then there are the many companies who get through the first two stages only to falter and fail later. In these instances, failure can often be traced to mistakes made during the start-up and takeoff stages. In other instances failure is attributable to a faulty concept and not to execution. If the original concept is faulty the company will fail no matter how good the CEO and his management team.

An outstanding concept, on the other hand, does not guaranty success no matter how poor the CEO. The failure of an outstanding idea can usually be traced directly to the CEO, and no one really wants to be remembered as the CEO who failed.

Five key responsibility areas for the CEO.

The CEO has many responsibilities, most of which, he delegates to others as the company grows. During the early stages the CEO will be required to assume many of these responsibilities. It is not unusual for the CEO of a start-up company to initially sell the product or service, perform direct labor operations, ship the product, and do clerical office work. These may not be the norm, but the CEO will be called upon to fill voids in the organization while it is in the formative stage.

Responsibilities of a CEO can be grouped into five "key responsibility" areas. These five key responsibility areas are:

1. Cash.

2. Strategy (including research and development).

3. Marketing.

4. Operations.

5. People.

Each key responsibility area is not static, since the emphasis within each area shifts as the company grows. For example, during the seed and start-up stage the emphasis should be on cash flow and the conservation of cash. In the growth and maturing stages the emphasis should be on the use of cash for strategic purposes.

The term "financial management" is not being used since it connotes a functional alignment of responsibilities. The company may eventually be organized functionally (engineering, manufacturing, marketing, finance, employee relations, legal etc.) to provide for efficient administration. The CEO, however, should have a broader view. He should focus his talent and time on the five key responsibility areas, which are interrelated and cut across functional lines of authority.

For example, responsibility for marketing will eventually be delegated to a Vice President of Marketing. Yet the CEO will always retain ultimate responsibility for success. He also will view the marketing process as requiring the participation of accounting, engineering and manufacturing.

Figure 2 lists the functions typically found in a fully developed manufacturing company. Engineering and Manufacturing can be combined to improve communications between these activities. Quality Control is often established as a function separate from Manufacturing. The CEO of a mature company rarely involves himself with the intimate details of every function.

The Entrepreneur as CEO deals with issues that are critical to success during each stage of a company's development. And these issues often cut across functional organizations.

The book has four parts, each devoted to one of the four stages of a company's life cycle. Each part is sub-divided into five sections dealing with the critical issues affecting the CEO's five key responsibility areas. Actions required to achieve success are spelled out in each section.

Emphasis is placed on the Seed & Start-up Stage, the Takeoff Stage and early aspects of the Growth Stage. Part 4, Beyond Growth, covers selected management issues of a maturing company. The mature company is more the province of the professional manager than the emerging entrepreneur.

The entrepreneur brings enthusiasm to the company, creates excitement, and has a vision for his enterprise. By coupling these positive attitudes with the actions outlined for each of the five key result areas (lessons gained from experience), the entrepreneur can enhance his prospects for success.

ORGANIZATION FUNCTIONS OF A
TYPICAL MANUFACTURING COMPANY.

Strategic Planning.
Research and Development.
    Projects and/or
    Physical sciences.
Engineering.
    Advanced engineering.
    Design engineering.
    Production engineering.
Manufacturing.
    Advanced manufacturing engineering.
    Manufacturing engineering.
    Quality control.
    Purchasing.
    Production control.
    Shop operations.
Marketing.
    Product planning.
    Sales.
    Product line management.
    Market research.
    Advertising and sales promotion.
    Distribution and warehousing.
Finance.
    Treasurer.
    Comptroller.
    Audit staff.
    Accounts payable.
    Accounts receivable.
    General accounting.
Legal.
    Patent attorney.
    Counsel.
Manpower.
    Employee relations.
    Organization and manpower development.

Figure 2

Many companies will have both a Chief Executive Officer and a Chief Operating Officer. The hypothesis used throughout the book is that the CEO and COO are alter egos of each other. Thus the five key responsibility areas are divided between the CEO and COO based on their individual strengths.

The board of directors, with the CEO and COO, can use the five key responsibility areas to assure that the CEO and COO have a clear understanding of those areas assigned to them. They also help define how the CEO and COO can best complement each other.

Leading by example.

In fulfilling these five key responsibilities there is one fact from which there is absolutely no escape and no reprieve. The CEO sets the example for every other person in the organization - no matter how large or small the company.

This is not a moral or philosophical issue. It is an unavoidable condition. Great CEO's know this and govern themselves accordingly. Perhaps this comes under the heading of leadership, one of several character and personal traits of successful CEO's beyond the scope of this book.

As used in this book, setting the example for others is an action item for the CEO. If the CEO is ostentatious or free with the way he spends the company's money, high living will become the norm. If the CEO tolerates poor quality, poor quality will become the norm. If the CEO views state and federal laws and regulations with contempt, contempt for laws and regulations will become the norm.

Aside from moral and ethical considerations, low standards can have a devastating financial impact on the company. The CEO sets the example, and eventually the company will be a reflection of him - and on him.

PART ONE

THE SEED AND START-UP STAGE.

Raising money.

The need for cash dominates the seed and start-up stage. A product involving a technology breakthrough may require several years of seed financing before the concept can be translated into a prototype. The principle distinction between seed financing and start-up financing is that seed money is typically used to prove the viability of a product or service, while start-up money is used to translate the concept into an ongoing business. The more typical product or service, which is the case considered here, can be brought to the prototype or demonstration stage fairly quickly after the entrepreneur has secured financing.

Unless the entrepreneur is able or willing to finance the seed and start-up stage himself, he will need to raise cash from private individuals or venture capital organizations. In raising cash, he will be required to relinquish some of his ownership so that investors can obtain a satisfactory return on their money. The entrepreneur should be careful how much ownership he relinquishes during the initial round of financing. Additional rounds are a virtual certainty and he will lose control of the company if he hasn't retained sufficient ownership.

The more fully developed the product or service concept the easier it will be to obtain financing under favorable terms. The entrepreneur should give serious consideration to using individual investors to finance development of a prototype or a demonstration site. With prototype in hand the entrepreneur can approach venture capital firms with greater confidence that he will obtain favorable terms.

To a certain extent the ownership issue is academic. Investors will base their ownership claim on the return they require from their investment, which has frequently been 40% per year.

If the company requires an investment of $1 million the venture capital firm will be seeking a valuation of approximately $5.5 million after five years. Multiplying the earnings in the fifth year by a PE ratio (price earnings ratio) and then by the percentage of ownership held by the venture capital firm determines the valuation.

For example, if the earnings in the fifth year are projected to be $2 million, and the venture capital firm owns 30% of the stock and they use a price earnings multiple of 10, their stock will have a projected valuation of $6 million. This meets their 40% ROI (Return On Investment) objective.

The controlling word in this formula is "projected", since there is no certainty the company will earn the projected income. This is one reason the venture capital firm will be seeking a high rate of return. Not all their investments are successful and they need winners to offset less successful investments.

Venture capital firms also frequently discount the earning projections and expect to see pro forma returns in excess of 50%. The entrepreneur should be careful that his projections are not too optimistic since he will lose credibility if results are not up to expectations. Credibility of an entrepreneur is an important factor in a venture capital firms decision to invest and to reinvest. It is not unusual for a start-up to require three or more rounds of financing before growth generates enough cash for the business to be self sustaining.

A proven track record with prior experience as a successful CEO, or other meaningful experience running a company, can enhance the credibility of the entrepreneur. Credibility is further enhanced when the caliber of the management team or choice of directors is outstanding. The entrepreneur usually can negotiate better terms when the investors have great confidence in him.

Negotiations for securing better terms from venture capital firms revolve around the "price earnings multiple", "return on investment" and the "credibility of the financial projections and management team".

If other companies with a related product went public at a price earnings multiple of 15, the entrepreneur should press for a multiple higher than ten times earnings. If the product is a very hot product with a high probability of success, the entrepreneur can press the investors to accept a lower rate of return. The entrepreneur also can stress where he has been conservative in the formulation of the financial projections. Whatever the negotiating strategy, it should be based on facts and enhance the credibility of the entrepreneur.

Fund raising goals.

The entrepreneur has three goals for his fund raising efforts.

First he must arouse interest in as many investors as possible. These can be venture capital firms or private investors. The greater the number of potential investors, the greater will be the probability of securing an investment under favorable terms from an investor favored by the entrepreneur.

Second, the entrepreneur needs to raise sufficient funds to reach his objective and be careful not to settle for too small an initial financing. The objective may be to complete successful testing of the prototype unit, get the product into production, or reach another milestone. Failure to achieve the objective for which the funds were raised will undermine the credibility of the management team. This can make it more difficult to raise additional funds on favorable terms.

Third he should obtain the funds while retaining majority ownership of the company.

Securing the funds is critical to launching the enterprise. Of equal importance is how the entrepreneur, turned CEO, uses those funds

Section One

Cash

Your most precious asset.

Cash during the early stages of a new company is the CEO's most precious asset. It is hard to raise, and easy to spend.

The CEO's first test occurs when he completes his initial financing. Cash in the bank has a beguiling effect and creates a false sense of security. Raising cash is a major effort, and completing a successful financing can create a heady atmosphere leading to wasteful spending. The euphoria created by "all that money in the bank" can lead to the use of cash for ego fulfilling purposes. Rationalizations occur, such as: "We need new furniture and it should be the best. This will allow customers and future investors to see we are a professional organization."

It is the CEO's job to guard against all such raids on the bank account. It is up to him to be certain the company's cash is spent wisely.

Figure 3 depicts the several claimants on cash. The first three account for the greatest cash usage during the seed and start-up stage.

People are frequently the greatest users of cash in any company. During the early stages people are likely to consume more cash than any other claimant.

Non-people engineering and R&D expense and non-people marketing expense also will represent major uses of cash during the seed and start-up stage.

CLAIMANTS ON CASH

People:
Salaries.   Benefits.
Phones.   Supplies.
Travel and living.

Marketing:
Research.   Advertising.
Promotions.   Displays.
Shows and exhibits.

Engineering and R&D:
Testing.   Patents.
Certifications.   Prototypes.
Specials.   New features.

Inventories:
Warehousing.   Obsolescence.
Freight.   Duties.
Letters of credit.

Receivables.

Figure 3

The time required to reach milestone objectives has an important bearing on cash usage. Delays in reaching these objectives can magnify the impact people have on cash usage. Obtaining UL approval, for example, is frequently an important milestone. It requires several months to complete and often results in unexpected delays. During this period, permanent employees must be paid. Hiring marketing or finance people prematurely, only to have them wait for UL or other approvals, is a cash drain. This can be a trap into which the CEO can easily fall. The meter is running while the clock keeps ticking.

Many such milestone objectives must be reached before the business can proceed. They can be shown on a CPM (critical path management) chart if time is taken to analyze the work that must be completed during the seed and start-up stage. Examples of critical milestones are; FCC approvals, FDA approvals, UL approvals, land use permits, and licenses.

Critical milestones such as these are usually identifiable ahead of time, although the time required to complete them is unknown and easily underestimated. Hidden critical milestones also must be addressed as they surface. Customer testing and recertification due to design changes are examples of hidden milestones.

Invariably it will take longer to complete each milestone than originally planned. These delays postpone introduction of the product or service and lengthens the seed and start-up stage.

Time is money, and delays affect the company in several ways. First there is the continuous cash drain during the period before sales begin. Second, competition may beat the company to market or take other actions that diffuse the impact of the company's product (diminishing its sales potential). Third, delayed introduction can result in a reduced market share. This can prevent the company from achieving the lower costs that should result from higher volume (based on learning curve theory).

It is important for the CEO to establish priorities to guide the company during each stage of the company's growth.

During the seed and start-up stage the emphasis, and priorities, should be on conserving cash while meeting critical milestone objectives. At this stage of the company's growth there are only a few employees. The small size of the organization makes it easier for the CEO to enlist support for his policy of cash conservation.

There are several actions the CEO can take to conserve cash while still meeting milestone objectives.

ACTIONS TO CONSIDER TAKING

1. Renting, instead of purchasing equipment.

Nearly everything needed by the company is available from rental companies. Three factors should influence the decision of whether to rent.

First is whether the equipment is required for temporary use. This is likely to be the case with engineering test equipment, where highly specialized equipment is needed for short, well defined periods of testing.

Second is the cost of purchase compared with the cost of rental. Rental fees are frequently between 8% and 12% of the purchase price of a new piece of equipment, plus the cost of shipping the equipment back to the rental company. Purchase of used equipment can often be justified if it can be obtained at 1/4 to 1/3 the price of new, and when usage is to extend well beyond three months. If used equipment at deep discounts is not available, then rental should be seriously considered.

Third is whether equipment requirements (features and specifications) have been well defined. Rental is often an excellent choice when it is uncertain which features or specifications are needed in a piece of equipment. Rental can provide the company an opportunity to try the equipment and verify that the equipment meets the company's needs. Computers are a case in point.

Fourth, some types of equipment have frequent model changes or steadily declining prices due to rapidly changing technology. Rental may be attractive under these conditions. FAX machines are an example.

2. Approve purchases before the fact.

The best time to establish approval routines is when the company is young. Waiting merely makes it more difficult to establish these routines. The longer that ad-hoc routines are allowed to exist the more difficult it is to convince people of the need for change. New approval routines also tend to encroach on individual prerogatives which increase natural resistance to change. Growth in the size of the organization will magnify the task of gaining acceptance of new approval routines.

The CEO will not want to burden the company with a plethora of bureaucratic routines, but he should recognize the importance of routines and establish priorities for their introduction. The routine for approving purchases should be among the first to be adopted.

It is not uncommon for a new CEO to sign all the checks for a young company, believing that by signing the checks he is controlling expenses. Signing checks is a good idea since it allows the CEO to know first hand where the money is going. It does not, however, control expenses. Commitments can be made by others in the company that obligate the CEO to pay the bill whether he wants to or not.

The only way to control expenses is to require approval of commitments (for purchases, travel, rentals, etc.) before they are made. This routine should also control the issuing of credit cards together with a procedure for approving employee expense accounts.

Initially the CEO can approve all such commitments, except for incidental supplies. People will not accept a routine that restricts their ability to do their job when small incidental purchases are involved. The procedure can specify that incidental supplies, up to a modest dollar limit, can be purchased without prior approval. Incidental purchases can be made using petty cash or by including the item on the employees' expense account.

The spirit behind the routine should encourage everyone to conserve cash and make every penny count, without forcing people to feel guilty about spending money on essentials.

As the company grows, the approval routine can be modified to delegate authority to approve commitments, within prescribed limits, to others in the company.

3. Use consultants and temporary employees.

During the seed and start-up stage every stratagem needs to be used to conserve cash. With people costs representing the major use of cash the CEO needs to pay particular attention to this area of expense.

Holding people costs to a minimum creates an apparent conflict between conserving cash and the need to hire the best available people as employees. If cash is the company's most precious asset, then people will be the company's most valuable resource.

It may be difficult for a seed and start-up company to attract the best people since the company represents a high risk for experienced, successful professionals. When it comes time to filling senior management or critical technical positions, the CEO should be prepared to offer solid compensation packages. It is usually not wise to scrimp on salary to hold down expenses if it means hiring less than the best.

Keeping the organization small during the seed and start-up stage conserves cash and encourages the company not to compromise on the quality of the people it hires. The obvious way to maintain a small organization and still meet scheduled milestone objectives is to use temporary employees, including consultants.

Most accounting and office tasks can be done with temporary clerks, typists, secretaries, and accountants. Many engineering tasks, from design to testing, can be done by consultants or by sub contracting the work to others. Market research can be done by consultants.

Consultants can be expensive. To keep consulting costs at a reasonable level it is important for assignments to be thoroughly defined before hiring the consultant. A poorly defined assignment results in the consultant taking time to define the work to be done in addition to accomplishing the desired task.

Cash can be saved by paying the consultant with company stock. Some consultants look favorably on this method of payment. It defers income and affords them an opportunity to earn the same 40% return (albeit with some risk involved) as the investors.

There are at least three advantages to using temporary employees, including consultants:

1. The company retains a specialist who can focus on the required task.

2. The company pays by the drink and avoids poor productivity resulting from an uneven workload, typical in a seed and start-up situation.

3. The company avoids locking itself into paying salaries and benefits should there be delays in completing milestone objectives, product development and product introduction.

There are some caveats when using consultants that deserve attention. First, and most obvious, is to be certain the consultant is qualified to do the job.

Second, the consultant may not have the same sense of urgency as the CEO or he may have other clients with demands on his time. If the consultant's assignment is part of the critical path, he should be contractually committed to a scheduled completion date and be monitored to assure the schedule is met.

Third, consultants may have a conflict of interest (not legally or ethically where they should disqualify themselves from the job) but one that inhibits them from accomplishing the desired objective. This can be the case when consultants interface with regulatory or licensing bodies from whom the company requires approvals. A consultant may be hesitant to place pressure on people with whom he must work in the future. A consultant can be very useful in guiding the company to the right people and in preparing the proper documents for submittal, but a member of management should retain responsibility for the interface.

The company also should explore the use of outside services besides temporary employees. The entire payroll activity, including the issuing of paychecks, withholding of taxes, insurance premiums and subsequent disbursement to the appropriate taxing authority or insurance company can be subcontracted to an outside service company or local bank.

The CEO should be aware that he is personally liable for employee withholding taxes. Having a responsible third party handle the payroll is a good way for the CEO to be certain withholding taxes are collected and paid to the government.

All outside services and agencies should be investigated to be certain they are financially sound and meet state laws, such as licensing for employee insurance coverage.

4. Avoid the trap of long term commitments.

Long term commitments lock the company into using its cash for a specific purpose at some future date, when the cash may be critically needed elsewhere. The company is contractually obligated to make payments on these long term commitments and has little, if any, discretion with respect to them.

Leasing and "rental to purchase agreements" should usually be avoided during the seed and start-up stage (though they may be very useful during the growth stage). The attraction of leasing and rental to purchase agreements is that they avoid a large cash outlay up front. They also provide a form of financing that might not otherwise be available (although the rates are usually very high). Avoiding the up front cash payment gives the appearance of conserving cash, but really doesn't do so since the company is contractually committed to make the payments.

Rental and lease payments as part of expense, are tax deductible. This has little meaning during the seed and start-up stage since the company probably will be in a cumulative loss position for the first few years. Cash in hand is more valuable than a future tax benefit, no matter what the present worth of the tax benefit. An accountant should be consulted for specific tax advice with respect to sub-chapter S corporations and for changes to the regulations.

If leasing space is unavoidable the best tactics will be to keep things simple and to retain as much flexibility with the space as possible. Most companies who produce a product begin by purchasing components and performing the assembly work themselves (or during the start-up stage having the entire product built by someone else). In either case warehouse type space is usually adequate for initial assembly and test operations.

Warehouse type space is also usually adequate for laboratory or engineering development work. A portion of the warehouse space can be made into inexpensive offices using movable partitions, without enclosed offices except a conference room. In this manner everything can be easily rearranged, or moved to another location, as the business grows.

Special power requirements, heavy lifting capabilities, ovens, plating or other environmentally sensitive processes can restrict flexibility. Every effort should be made during the start-up stage to farm out work requiring equipment of this type. Final space and investment decisions involving these kinds of equipment should be deferred until the next stage when management has a better fix on the company's needs.

5. Perils of hiring too many people, too soon.

As described earlier, consultants and temporary help can minimize payroll costs: But hiring people too soon also can create a poor work environment.

When a key person is hired (such as the Vice President of Manufacturing, Marketing or Finance) he is going to want to do the job for which he has been hired. The CEO should be in a position to allow him to do it.

During the seed and start-up stage the work load in each function will be uneven. If every key position is filled there won't be enough work to keep key people busy. If they are good people they won't sit around waiting for something to do but will begin working on projects needed in the future. At best, these efforts will be premature (and may need to be redone) while diverting attention away from achieving critical milestone objectives.

It's always worth remembering Parkinson's Law (see appendix), that "work expands so as to fill the time available for its completion." Using cash for anything other than essential tasks during this stage is a serious mistake.

6. Silence the siren song of extravagance.

A necessity to one person can be considered an extravagance to another, and when egos are involved it is often difficult to distinguish between necessity and extravagance. The CEO must take a firm stand, make the distinction and prevent any semblance of extravagance. He can do this best by setting the example.

The following is a list of what can easily be classified as extravagances for a company in the seed and start-up stage.

- Company cars for executives or employees.

- Cellular telephones.

- First class air travel.

- Hotel suites.

- Memberships in clubs or organizations.

- Fancy offices, including excess space.

- Individual secretaries.

There are many other not so visible extravagances, where a little attention can result in important savings.

- Telephone credit cards. To be avoided except where extensive travel warrant their use.

- Interest payments on payables. This is usually very expensive credit at 1 1/2% per month, or 18% per year. It can be avoided by paying the bill on time or by not doing business with suppliers who charge interest.

- Personalized stationary, memo pads etc. can be avoided entirely. Office supplies also can be purchased from discount houses such as the Office Club. A memo imprinted "From the desk of . . ." is no more effective than a plain note. On the other hand, constantly running out of supplies is a waste of time and is not cost effective.

In taking a strong stand on extravagance and unnecessary expenses the CEO should be careful not to become obsessed by cost cutting. Cost cutting shouldn't obstruct getting the job done.

Section Two

Strategy

Eleven critical questions.

A complete strategic plan includes an evaluation of every facet of the business and of the environment (economic and political) in which the business operates. It establishes the actions required of the company to achieve success.

The strategic planning process involves an analysis of the strengths and weaknesses of the company and its competitors, which provides a basis for the action plan.

Every large established business should have evolved such a plan over a period of years.

The CEO of a seed and start-up company cannot afford the time and effort required to produce such a comprehensive plan. He must still prepare a business plan that incorporates the key elements of a full-fledged strategic plan. The business plan he develops will allow the CEO to explain his business to potential investors and bankers and provide a base line against which to measure results. Updated on an annual basis the business plan becomes a living document helping the CEO to refine his strategy (or tactics) as he and the company gain experience in the marketplace.

In preparing the initial plan the following questions should be addressed.

1. What is the market or market niche the product or service will serve? How large is the market or market niche?

2. What are competing products and technologies? What are the strengths and weaknesses of the company's

new product versus competing products and technologies?

3. What are the prices of competing products or services? At what price will the company's new product or service be sold (initially and longer term)?

4. Who are the competitors? What are their strengths and weaknesses? How do they go to market?

5. What major competitive advantage will the company's new product or service have over the competition?

6. Are there any environmental issues that can impact the new product or service?

7a. (For a product manufacturing business.) How will the new product be manufactured? What will it cost? Can manufacturing be farmed out, and if so where?

7b. (For a service business.) What is the scope of the service to be offered? How will the service be delivered or performed? What is the cost of providing the service?

8. What sales volume can be achieved over the next five years? What costs will be incurred? What will be the gross margin?

9. What market share will the product or service capture? Is it realistic?

10. What are the cash requirements of the business over the five year forecast period?

11. What key people will be required? From where will they come?

In determining whether any additional questions need to be answered, the CEO should identify any issue that could have a major near term impact on the company. These "what if" questions are usually most meaningful for a new company over the near term (perhaps a year). Later, after the company reaches the growth stage, longer range issues can be explored.

An area of planning that can easily be overlooked is whether there is an emerging technology that will compete with the company's product or service. Emerging technologies, by their nature, are not readily apparent and the effort to search for them may seem like a waste of time. Learning about a new technology that could make the company's product obsolete may be unpleasant, but it's better to find out about the technology now rather than after considerable money has been spent. Early knowledge of a competing technology also may permit changes in design, distribution, pricing or other aspects of the business, when it is easier and less costly to make a change.

The Pony Express was an exciting and imaginative venture, but the telegraph was quicker and safer. Similarly, the canal builders of the early nineteenth century could not compete against the railroads.

Today's rapid advancements in technology make this aspect of the planning job more than cause for casual concern. Consider the rapid evolution of the common printer, from a basic typewriter mechanism, to the daisywheel, dot matrix, and laser printers.

Linking six sub-strategies.

A simple and effective approach to the planning process for a new company is to link strategies for each key planning element together to form an integrated total strategy.

For most companies the following represents the key elements for which strategies should be developed and around which the business plan can be written.

1. Cash strategy.

2. Marketing strategy.

3. Production or service delivery strategy.

4. Manpower strategy.

5. R&D strategy.

6. Resource analysis.

These are at the core of most decisions that will decide the success or failure of a business. If there are other factors critical to success they can be added to the above list. If, for example, it is important to secure FDA approval a "regulatory approval strategy" can be added.

■   <u>Cash strategy.</u>

The CEO of a seed and start-up company who wishes to retain control of the company could define his cash strategy as follows: "Use private sources for initial financing of product development. Venture capital will be obtained after demonstrating the success of the product. Bank loans will be used for working capital, using inventories and receivables as collateral. Public financing (Initial Public Offering) will be used to finance growth."

Relying solely on private capital to develop the product and bring it to market, depends on adequate sources of private capital and the ability to produce the product with a minimum investment. This cash strategy may limit growth. If rapid growth and market share are critical to success this may not be a good cash strategy.

Another strategy could involve venture capital financing while the product is still under development, and include multiple rounds of financing.

A third strategy could involve the establishment of separate distribution companies in foreign countries and issuing an I.P.O. in each country, using the proceeds to fund growth.

A fourth cash strategy could be to use private and venture capital to establish a demonstration site, such as with a retail or service business. Franchising would then be used to fund growth.

Cash flow projections based on the marketing, production and R&D strategies provide the starting point for development of the cash strategy.

■ Marketing strategy.

The development of a marketing strategy, which encompasses distribution, sales, advertising, pricing, and product planning, will depend on the answers to questions concerning the competition, competing products or services, and the major advantage that the company's product has over the competition's.

How to differentiate the product and to position it within a market or market niche is a key element of the marketing strategy. Other questions that also must be answered by the marketing strategy include:

(a) Which distribution channel will give the company a competitive advantage or provide competitive service at the lowest cost?

(b) What is the best sales strategy for the product?

(c) What should be the role of after sales service?

(d) What should be the pricing strategy?

The objectives to be achieved by the strategy also should be stated. Obtaining initial orders is an important early objective for every start-up company. Sales projections covering the five year forecast period also should be prepared and represent the financial expression of the marketing strategy.

■ Production strategy.

At the core of this strategy will be answers to the following questions. Who will make the product? Where will the product be made? How will quality be maintained?

In determining who will make the product it will be necessary to establish, (1) the importance of making the product in house versus farming out production, (2) the amount of cash that can be allocated to manufacturing instead of to engineering or marketing, and (3) the difference in cost between farming out production versus making the product in house.

These same factors apply to components and assemblies as well as to the complete product. An important and proprietary component can be made in house for incorporation into the finished product by someone else: Or all parts and components can be made by someone else and assembled in house: Or operations involving high cost equipment or dangerous processes can be farmed out and the remainder of the work done in house: Or the entire product can be built by someone else.

When deciding where to make the product consideration should be given to all alternatives including the United States, the Far East, the Caribbean, and Mexico.

Maintaining quality is a key element in the production strategy and can be an important factor in deciding where to make the product.

The following describes a hypothetical production strategy. "The entire product will be manufactured by a supplier located in the United States in proximity to our company, until customers have accepted the product and all design and quality problems have been overcome. During this period we expect to incur a cost penalty over having the product built in house or in the Far East. After this period of initial production, assembly and test will be brought in house. Component parts and certain subassemblies will be purchased offshore from low cost producers who can meet our quality requirements."

The production strategy is interlocked with the cash strategy and with the marketing strategy.

A service company will have somewhat different questions that need to be answered when formulating its "service delivery" strategy.

A product service company that repairs and maintains equipment will, for example, need to decide whether the service will be performed at the company's premises or on-site at the customers premises, or both? On-site service requires a logistics system to deliver the service technician with spare parts and test equipment to the customers location, when needed. The marketing and cash strategies will determine whether the company should develop an on-site service capability.

■   Manpower strategy.

The primary need of any new company is to fill the gaps in experience or skills that exist in the original management team. The marketing, cash and production strategies will identify other manpower needs.

■ Research and development strategy.

For the seed and start-up company the major issues are likely to be (1) how much additional development work is required before entering production, and (2) how to effectively transition the product from R&D to production.

The marketing strategy will define new products and features on which R&D may be required to work.

■ Resource analysis.

The CEO must critically evaluate the availability of resources and be certain sufficient of them are available to carry out the strategic plan. Cash and people are typically the limiting resources at this stage of the company's development.

Cash flow projections can provide an insight into the adequacy of cash.

The adequacy or availability of manpower resources is more difficult to judge. A high technology service business, such as computer services, can have its growth restricted by the lack of trained service technicians. Turnover can be a serious problem that is difficult to forecast, except where industries have had a history of high turnover.

Systems, inherent to management control, will eventually become a major issue as volume increases. Systems and the availability of materials can easily become limiting items as the company enters the takeoff or growth stages.

As with the other key responsibility areas (Cash, Marketing, Operations and People) there are actions the CEO should consider taking and actions that he should avoid.

ACTIONS TO CONSIDER TAKING.

1. Keep the design focused.

Engineering must concentrate on completing the development of the initial product to be brought to market. Allowing engineering to deviate from this objective can delay introduction of the initial product and result in the unplanned expenditure of cash.

The original product description, to which engineering is working, establishes the features and specifications for the product, which gives the product certain attributes and capabilities. It is not unusual for someone to suggest modifying the products' capabilities or features when the design is nearing completion. The idea can originate in engineering based on work they have been doing, or it can originate in marketing as the result of discussions with potential customers. No matter where the idea originates the CEO must be adamant in his position not to allow engineering to deviate from the original plan; unless he is convinced that the changes are essential to gaining customer acceptance of the product.

This can be one of the most important decisions a CEO can make in a start-up situation. Introducing a product that will not meet customer requirements is obviously a mistake. Not as obvious, is the drain on cash caused by delay. The wrong decision can easily bankrupt the company.

Typically the suggestion will be made that a change can be made without incurring any additional cost or causing any delay in introducing the product. These assertions will nearly always be wrong. A change, no matter how small, usually impacts the design in some unexpected manner, causing revisions that frequently cause additional revisions. Although it may be unfair to categorize these suggestions as last minute ideas, the fact remains that they probably haven't been well thought through and had the benefit of thorough analysis.

The other mechanism that creates delay is the tendency for engineering to want to improve what they have already done. These are creeping changes where, with just a little more tinkering the design can be improved upon. Engineers should be commended for their desire to do outstanding and professional work, but need to be reminded that completing the work on time may be more important than marginal improvements. Engineering should document ideas for improving the original design later.

Product improvement ideas should be saved for the first product redesign, by which time marketing and customers will have suggested additional changes based on actual field experience.

2. Know when to freeze the design.

A corollary to the axiom of keeping engineering focused on completing the design, is to know when to freeze the design. Engineering will always be looking for the latest advancement in technology and attempt to see how it can improve the design. A new integrated circuit or faster FET that can operate at higher temperatures, for example, may have the potential for reducing the number of components and result in lower costs. However, refining the design to incorporate the latest advancement can delay introduction of the product, reduce needed revenues and consume cash.

The design must be frozen at some point otherwise engineering will be following the design to the factory floor, which is an impossible situation.

The time to freeze the design is when it meets the original design specifications, is reliable and producible. It's the responsibility of the CEO to see that this happens.

3. Assure adequate testing.

Incomplete testing can kill a product (and a new company) before it can get off the ground. Going to market with a product that doesn't work as advertised, or that has a high failure rate is the kiss of death. This is especially true for a new company that is trying to establish itself.

The CEO should approve the test plan and not release the product to production until satisfied that the product is reliable and meets specifications. Units from a preproduction run should be tested to verify that the design has been properly transferred to operations.

4. Limit the number of initial models.

During the start-up stage it is important not to introduce too many models at once or to change designs too frequently.

Too many configurations of a basic design dissipate resources and increase engineering, inventory, distribution and production costs. The marketing plan should define the models required initially to serve the market. Later, during the growth stage, a marketing strategy calling for the rapid introduction of new models is frequently an excellent move. It is not wise to undertake such a strategy too soon.

Frequent design changes also can have a negative impact on costs, and result in obsolete inventory and service problems. Every design change, no matter how small, affects engineering and production and places a burden on systems that are not yet well established. If systems become overloaded the company can fall like a house of cards.

The two forces that will be pressing for change are marketing and the need to reduce costs. Marketing will want changes to meet special customer requests and everyone will be suggesting ways to reduce the cost of the product.

The CEO must have control over these decisions otherwise all the good ideas for product improvements and cost reductions will turn into a bad idea for the company.

Section Three

Marketing

Initial direction for Marketing.

Marketing is critical to the success of the company and deserves the best talent available. It may not, however, be wise to appoint a Vice President of Marketing until the product is nearly ready for introduction. The CEO should have a clear picture in mind of the marketing work that needs to be done during the seed and start-up stage and establish a schedule for completing this work. Hiring a Marketing VP too soon may not be the best use of cash and result in much wheel spinning. If the CEO has had marketing or sales experience he should take the lead and perform the role of the Marketing VP. If he is not strong in marketing he will need to augment this void in his capabilities.

One of the other founders may be experienced in marketing and fill this void until it is appropriate to hire a Marketing VP. If this is not possible the CEO can appoint a person with an extensive marketing background to the board of directors with the understanding that he will provide the company with the necessary guidance and marketing savvy.

During the seed and start-up stage emphasis should be placed on defining the market, determining how to differentiate the product, obtaining initial orders for beta site or product testing, and determining how to market the product.

The classic model for starting a business is to identify a need and find a better way to fill it. Care should be taken that there is a real need for a product based on a new technology.

There are times when the technology itself becomes so alluring that it is assumed there is a need for the technology.

When this happens the company finds itself with a solution looking for a problem.

An excellent example of this was a lighting technology based on high frequency excitation of plasma and phosphors to create a compact fluorescent light bulb. The high frequency fluorescent bulb used one third the energy of a standard incandescent light bulb, and because of its small round size, allowed the light to be focused.

No other small fluorescent lamps were available at the time the new technology was first developed. The investors believed that the energy savings of the new technology would create a market for the high frequency compact fluorescent lamp. The high cost of making the new lamp made it uneconomical for several years. When the lamp was ready to be introduced, other low cost, energy saving compact fluorescent lamps using conventional fluorescent technology, were on the market. The high frequency technology had been preempted by conventional technology.

There is still no verifiable need for the high frequency fluorescent lamp, though the technology may still have potential. The ability to focus light is still a superior feature over standard fluorescent lamps.

It is important, therefore, to be certain that there really is a need for a new technology before spending much time and money on developing the product. Market research can be a valuable tool for deciding whether a market exists and for positioning the product if it is decided to proceed with development.

ACTIONS TO CONSIDER TAKING.

1. Get seven answers from your market study.

A well executed market study will provide insights and information that make it possible to reach sound decisions. The study should establish or verify:

1. Market attractiveness.

2. Product acceptability, including the value that customers place on the benefits ascribed to the product.

3. The strengths and weaknesses of competitors and their products.

4. Competitive pricing levels.

5. Distribution channels used by competitors.

6. Names of the best distributors and manufacturers representatives.

7. List of prospects who would be the most likely initial customers or who would be best suited for beta site tests.

2. Cover seven essentials in the marketing plan.

The marketing plan is a natural outgrowth of the marketing strategy and establishes how the strategy will be implemented. The marketing plan should describe in detail:

1. How to differentiate the product from the competition's and how the customer benefits from the differentiation.

2. The targeted market or niche, and the targeted customers.

3. How the product will be introduced and sold.

4. How the product will be distributed.

5. How the product will be priced.

6. How the product will be serviced.

7. The product warranty.

Two caveats about the marketing plan. It should not be wordy or lengthy. And it should be realistic.

3. Know all your constituencies.

Introducing a new product involves the development of a constituency much the same as a politician must do. One way of visualizing this process is to picture a stone being thrown into the ocean (which represents the market). When the stone hits the water it creates waves that emanate outward from the epicenter of the disturbance.

In our case the stone is the product idea. At the center of the disturbance are the founders who are convinced their product will be a success. Immediately outward from them are the company's employees, who must be sold on the worth of the endeavor to elicit their enthusiasm and hard work. Next are the investors who must be convinced that the product can succeed and adds value to the market.

Further out the waves created by the new product involve an ever widening group of constituents: Third parties who have tested the product such as at beta test sites: Industry consultants and market researchers who have evaluated the product: Distributors and suppliers who believe enough in the product to commit their resources to it: The technical and trade press who have spoken with the third parties testing the product and with industry consultants and market researchers so that they can write about the product and the company: The business press and financial analysts who investigate and report on how well the company and its products are performing.

Finally, at the outermost circle of constituents (see figure 4), are potential customers who rely on the comments and judgements of the others who have tested, analyzed or evaluated the product and the company.

An effective sales plan will assure the development of as many of these constituencies as possible.

The market study should identify who make up these constituencies and how the competition goes to market. Studying competitors market channels can help identify the constituencies who comprise the influence channels.

An example is the commercial segment of the lighting industry where contractors purchase the lighting fixtures, which determines the type of lamps or bulbs that will be used. In this situation the building will be designed by architects and engineers for the building owner. Though the building owner is the ultimate buyer he probably will not be the person who will decide which lighting product to use. Lighting specialists, architects, distributors and contractors will play key roles in the purchasing decision and each of these constituencies must be addressed in the sales plan.

In this situation the lighting specialist must be educated on the characteristics of the lighting product. These include color rendering properties, amount of light generated, focus or spread of the light, first cost, energy usage or savings, and life of the product. Once convinced that the attributes of the lighting product will serve the buildings' requirements he can recommend the product to the architect.

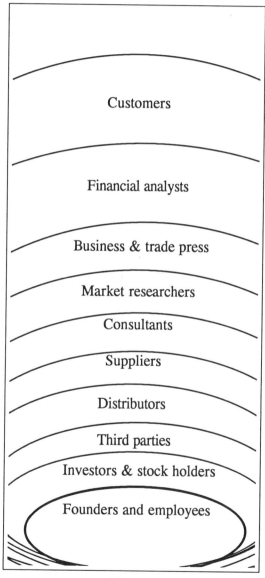

Customers

Financial analysts

Business & trade press

Market researchers

Consultants

Suppliers

Distributors

Third parties

Investors & stock holders

Founders and employees

Figure 4

In a like manner the architect must be convinced that a new lighting product will meet his requirements, in which case he may specify the product in his drawings.

The contractor will attempt to meet the architect's specifications but also will look for lower cost alternatives. He also will want to buy the lighting product from the distributor supplying him with his other electrical needs and will want the distributor to stock the product until it is needed at the construction site. The distributor can recommend alternative products and provide reasons as to why the cheaper alternatives are equal to the product specified by the architect.

Throughout this process it is important for all constituencies to become advocates for the product, especially if it is a unique product sold at a premium price. If the product in question saves energy but has a higher first cost than competing products, the lighting specialist, the architect and the building owner must all be sufficiently convinced of the value of the product for them to insist on its installation, even if the contractor or distributor suggests alternatives with lower first costs.

While commercial products confront certain distribution challenges, such as those described for lighting products, other markets will have different challenges. Jobbers and shelf space in the consumer market: Marine architects in the marine market: Consultants in the telecommunications market, etc..

Reaching all the constituencies and convincing them of the benefits of the product or service, is the purpose of the sales plan and the plan for introducing the product.

4. Select your distribution channel, carefully.

The market study will have identified distribution alternatives and the best distributors or manufacturers representatives, while the sales plan will have established the best channel for the product.

No matter what the product, existing channels or major portions of the channel may already be committed to other products. Distributors and manufacturers representatives, for example, can only handle a limited number of products. Large competitors may have taken actions that lock important portions of the distribution channel into only carrying their products.

It is unlikely that the company can initially afford a large direct sales force. Lack of available distributors, manufacturers representatives etc. can be a barrier to entering the market. The CEO needs to determine the seriousness of this issue as early as possible. If existing channels are closed to the company, the CEO will need to develop a strategy for overcoming the problem. One such strategy could be a strategic alliance with another company that already has an effective marketing organization with an established channel of distribution.

5. Get those all important initial orders.

It is very important to obtain sufficient initial orders to achieve two objectives.

The first objective is to prove the reliability and performance of the product under actual operating conditions. This helps assure that there are no undetected quality, reliability or performance problems. It also results in the development of customers to whom future prospects, consultants and the trade press can be referred for unbiased product information.

Initial orders can provide the CEO with an opportunity to obtain first hand feedback about the product and how customers feel toward it. Even if no serious problems arise at the beta or demonstration sites (which hopefully will be the case), the feedback can help in the preparation of communications programs and in evaluating the validity of the sales and distribution plans.

The second objective will be to prove to the investors (existing and potential) that the product really can be sold and that the assumptions used in the business plan, concerning marketability and price are valid.

It is frightening how much reassurance investors need that the product will sell. The initial orders provide the reassurance investors look for, and makes it more likely that they will continue to invest on terms that are favorable to the company.

The CEO should be an active participant in selecting the customers who should be targeted for these initial sales, in selling the product and in following up after installation. The CEO also should decide when to initiate the sales effort since it can be very damaging if it starts too soon. Delay in delivering the product will be construed negatively by the customer and can give the product and company a bad reputation. This is true whether the delay is merely due to not having sufficient product or whether it is caused by design or production problems. Premature announcements are also to be avoided. Bad press can cripple a company's ability to sell its product long after a problem is solved.

Initial customers represent important early constituencies the company needs to cultivate.

The CEO must be certain the product is ready and that delivery promises can be kept before the company begins its initial sales effort or initial publicity campaign. Furthermore, initial orders should only be taken for low risk installations, where delays or product problems won't hurt the customer.

Not withstanding this, some products can be market tested without incurring negative consequences. Consumer products are routinely tested in this manner. In addition it is frequently possible to work with a single customer on a strictly developmental basis, where it is clear to both parties that the product is undergoing development while installed at the customer's site. These approaches provide additional information about the product and its probable acceptance by customers.

6. Prepare contract documents.

Preparation of contract documents is an activity that is often an afterthought and relegated to a position of secondary importance. As a result, it doesn't receive the attention it deserves.

The CEO should make it a point to have contract documents prepared before undertaking the initial sales effort. Some documents requiring attention, include:

(a) Sales contracts.

(b) Warranty.

(c) Distributor or manufacturer representatives agreements.

Preparing these documents is not a terribly difficult task. These documents often represent statements of policy (such as with product warranties) and require the attention of the CEO. Copies of relevant documents containing terms that are typical for the industry can be obtained from customers. These can be used as a starting point for drafting the company's documents, which can then be completed by an attorney.

These documents should provide the company with the maximum protection while still being acceptable to customers. It is always possible to modify the documents on a case by case basis to conform with specific competitive situations. The CEO should retain control over approving changes during the early stages of the company's existence.

The CEO should be alert to the fact (and obtain guidance from his attorney concerning this subject) that omitting a topic from a contract document does not exclude the topic from the contract and thereby protect the company. Every state has a legal code covering commercial dealings. These codes establish the contract terms when the contract document is silent. They cover most situations that can arise in a commercial transaction.

The terms contained in the code may prevail if the contract document doesn't modify them. Omitting a topic, such as the terms of a warranty, can place the seller at a disadvantage since the uniform commercial code usually protects the buyer. The lack of a contract document or coverage of a topic may place the company at the mercy of every state's commercial code, with potentially disastrous results.

The company also should be aware that when doing business with the government, many contract terms are established by law. Taking exception to these terms can result in the company's proposal being declared non-responsive. Some onerous terms in a government contract are not stipulated by law. Exception may be taken to these terms if they represent an undue risk to the company. The proposal may still be declared non-responsive if a competitor did not take exception to the terms. Special consideration should be given to obtaining expert assistance concerning contract terms if the company expects to do considerable business with the government.

7. Hiring the first marketing employee.

The timing of this hire will depend on whether a founder is filling the position of Marketing Vice President. If so, he may be able to do most of the support work until the marketing effort gets underway in earnest. If not, the CEO will require some help as he begins to secure the initial crucial orders. This will definitely be the case if the product is technical in nature or potential customers conduct evaluations. In these instances customer's will need to contact a person other than the CEO, to obtain necessary product information and answers to technical questions.

It is very likely that this will be the beginning of the inside sales organization.

8. Beware of premature promotion.

As discussed earlier, the CEO needs to be certain that marketing does not get ahead of the company's ability to deliver at this early stage of the company's development. Hiring marketing people too soon not only drains cash but is likely to guarantee premature promotion of the product or service.

9. Avoid premature distribution agreements.

It is difficult to know with certainty during the seed and start-up stage whether the distribution and sales plan, as originally postulated, represents the best approach for the company. In addition the company will want to engage the best team of distributors, dealers or manufacturer representatives that it can attract.

It behooves the company to take sufficient time to search out the distributors, etc., who form the right channel and are best for the company. Distributors and manufacturer representatives also will want to start representing the company immediately when they sign their agreement. Again it is important to be certain the product is ready before moving ahead with the agreements.

This delay, however, may contradict the natural inclination of a Marketing Vice President who will want to establish a national distribution channel (assuming a product to be sold nationally) as quickly as possible. It takes time to establish a good distribution channel and the Marketing Vice President, recognizing this, may be over anxious to sign distribution agreements. This will be an area of concern for the CEO and the subject should be thoroughly aired to be certain the right decisions are made.

Section Four

Operations

Excellence in execution.

Operations equals execution - and the CEO must assure the quality of execution.

The CEO will find it necessary to delegate day to day operations. His attention will rightfully be focused on cash flow, on investors and banking, on marketing and on being certain the product is ready for sale.

The operating side of the business also usually involves a myriad of details requiring full time attention. The challenge for the CEO is to assure that execution is excellent, while not becoming embroiled in details.

Delegation requires clearly defined goals (schedules etc.) and a vehicle for following up to determine whether goals are being achieved, and if not, to assure that corrective actions are taken.

It is usually better to hire an experienced operating manager, though it is possible that the person responsible for R&D is also qualified as a manager of operations. Yet, in a start-up, Research and Development has done the engineering work (design etc.) and its manager probably will need to continue working on advanced designs of the original product or new products. It is also unlikely that the same person can manage Operations and R&D simultaneously.

The CEO also should recognize the need for separating design and production engineering from R&D, and for integrating these activities with manufacturing. The reason for this is that the CEO must be certain that key objectives are met when moving the product from development to production, specifically:

1. That the documentation required for production is complete and that there is strict control over documentation.

2. That the product is producible and is not subject to continuing change to satisfy incremental design improvements.

3. That R&D retains its focus on developing the next generation of product or on the strategic objective assigned to R&D.

Separating Operations from R&D establishes checks and balances that will help the CEO be certain that the transition from R&D to production is effective. Combining operations with R&D could drive one or the other function to a lower level in the organization. This would make it more difficult for the CEO to know what is happening in the organization, create an unnecessary organization layer and make one function appear to be less important than the other.

An alternative to hiring a Manager of Operations is to employ a consulting firm to do most of the initial production work. Consulting firms can prepare the documentation and arrange for the initial manufacture of the product by outside firms.

The reverse is also possible, since the company could have hired a consulting firm to do the R&D work. When subcontracting R&D work it is important for the contract to define the work to be done and the documentation and information to be delivered to the company. Operations require a clearly defined point of departure otherwise considerable time can be spent clarifying the work done by the R&D consulting firm.

During the seed and start-up stage, operating emphasis will be on moving the product from R&D to production, and the CEO should consider the following actions.

ACTIONS TO CONSIDER TAKING.

1. Assure complete documentation.

When freezing the design it is essential to prepare a complete set of documentation. This documentation should represent the product as it is to be built and should reflect the configuration that has been tested.

Preproduction units should be built using this documentation and these units also should be tested (as part of the product testing program described earlier). The preproduction run should identify producibility issues that were not previously recognized, such as process limitations, tolerance buildups, drawing errors and operations that interfere with each other.

The CEO cannot permit the product to be released for production until the documentation is complete and until the testing of the preproduction run units proves the integrity of the design and that the design is producible.

The required documentation usually includes:

(a) Complete bill of materials.

(b) Drawings.

(c) Specifications for components and parts, including sources for critical items.

When a company is to be a service and not a manufacturing business, the CEO must assure himself that the capabilities for delivering the service are in place.

In some respects this is more difficult than dealing with a product because judgement is needed when defining the required capabilities. If, for example, the business is to repair personal computers, a judgement must be made as to what spare components to maintain in inventory and what test equipment to have on hand. These decisions will be based on an estimate of the makes and models that are likely to be brought in for repair and service. In spite of taking great care in making the estimate, a computer will probably be brought in for repair for which the company will not have spare parts or test equipment. Under these circumstances the company must decide whether to attempt to repair the unit, and under what terms and conditions it will offer to do the work. If this happens occasionally it will not be a major problem. If it happens frequently it suggests that the company may not have understood its market.

Service businesses require that the scope of the service offering be carefully thought through and documented. This should be done when preparing the business plan since many subsequent decisions depend on the precise definition of the service to be performed. For the personal computer service business, the makes to be serviced should be decided ahead of time, so that the investment in parts, test equipment and training can be concentrated on these units. If the market has been properly researched and intelligent choices made with respect to operating decisions, such as parts inventories, the CEO can have some confidence that the company will be able to perform as advertised.

2. Establish an aggressive quality plan.

The first step in assuring product quality is to complete the documentation, preproduction run, testing and producibility engineering (or the service plan for a service business).

The CEO should describe to operations the principles on which he wants the quality plan to be predicated. The following three principles can lead to excellence in quality.

1. Zero defects.

2. Commitments from everyone to do their best.

3. Constant improvement.

Few products or services are perfect so the first principle can appear to be unrealistic and smack of Pollyanna. Zero defects is still an objective toward which everyone can strive. "Quality is Free" by Philip B. Crosby advocates this idea and establishes a strong case for it.

Interestingly the General Electric Company promulgated an approach to quality during the 1950's that placed the emphasis on preventing defects rather than catching them. But the controlling factor was the "cost of quality", not the best quality possible.

The GE approach equated the cost of preventing quality problems against the sum of appraisal costs plus failure costs (including warranty failures). Prevention included such activities as quality control engineering, preproduction runs and training. Appraisal costs included inspection and test. Failure costs included test failures and warranty costs.

It reasoned that the most cost effective quality system would emerge from this approach. The lowest quality cost would be reached when prevention costs were balanced against other quality costs. That is, when "Cost of prevention = Cost of appraisal + Cost of failures."

The emphasis placed on prevention was excellent, but by using quality costs as the controlling factor, the concept interjected two serious drawbacks. First it implied that poor quality was acceptable by saying there was a level of failure costs (equal to prevention costs minus appraisal costs) that would be tolerated by management. Second, for practical reasons, it only included warranty costs as a component of failure costs. It did not include other costs incurred by the customer; or the loss of customer trust and confidence resulting from failure of the product.

The principle of zero defects forces the organization to strive for perfection and may result in prevention costs far exceeding the costs of appraisal and failure. It will, however, eventually pay for itself in greater customer acceptance and, probably, in lower "total quality costs" as the product and manufacturing process are improved.

The second principle now comes into play; where everyone does his best to reach the objective of zero defects.

The current GE concept at appliance park in Louisville Kentucky, allows the worker who is not satisfied with quality to shut down the production line. Getting everyone to do their best enhances the goal of zero defects.

Finally if truly excellent quality and superior products are to be achieved, the quality of the product must be constantly improved. Improvements can result from improved processes, tighter standards, design improvements and worker care. For the product to be the best in the marketplace, the standards used for design, test and measurement must be superior to those used by competitors for their products.

Toughness on the part of the CEO can avert a catastrophe for the company. A case in point was a start-up company that began manufacturing its product before the product was ready for production. The board hired a new CEO after the company started production. He quickly determined that the product did not meet three important specifications (relating to FCC requirements, audible noise emanating from the product and obtaining UL approval). Production was immediately stopped, but only after 8,000 units were built and shipped. If production had been allowed to continue the rate would have increased to 10,000 units per month. Subsequently it also was determined that half the product line (the half that incorporated automatic control using power line carrier technology) could not meet performance criteria and required extensive development.

Based on this information the board of directors decided to exit the business. A post script to this horror story was that many of the original 8000 units failed after being in service for several months.

Shutting down production and then exiting the business was traumatic and costly. But it was not the financial disaster that would have occurred if the company had continued in production and installed 100,000 or more units only to have a high percentage fail.

3. Define the production strategy.

The CEO will need to develop a production strategy with the person responsible for operations. The initial strategy will hinge on how much work is to be farmed out, for which there are essentially four alternatives.

1. Farm out the manufacture of the product in its entirety; from procurement of materials through final assembly and test.

2. Farm out all work except final assembly and test.

3. Farm out specific processes or subassemblies while performing the balance of the work in house.

4. Do the complete manufacturing job in house.

The production strategy should be explicit for the start-up stage, define the probable direction it will take during the takeoff stage, and leave the longer range production strategy for later definition (other than to suggest concepts that may be of strategic importance to the company).

An example for a service company or franchise business might be to define precisely where the initial locations will be established. Then define geographic priorities for future locations, once the business is in the takeoff stage.

4. Defer major investments.

Conserving cash and maintaining flexibility are two overriding considerations during the seed and start-up stage.

The issue during the early stages of the company is how much cash to use for plant and equipment and to what extent these cash outlays limit future choices.

Production tooling in the form of molds, dies and forms may be a good investment if design changes wont affect the tooling. Their cost (if not purchased outright) will be amortized, by the supplier, and included in his price. The question is whether to pay for the tooling now or pay later.

Purchasing the tooling outright allows flexibility in choosing suppliers and keeps the supplier from having an unfair pricing advantage when the company places repeat orders. If the supplier raises his price the company can transfer the tooling to a more responsive supplier. The company also retains control over the ability of the supplier to sell parts made from the company's tooling to a third party. This could be extremely important if the part is proprietary or if the company doesn't want third parties (such as independent service companies) purchasing the parts directly from its supplier.

An example of where this occurred: turbine manufacturers sub-contracted the manufacture of turbine buckets but did not purchase the tooling. The suppliers, claiming that the product was theirs to sell to whom ever they wished, sold buckets to independent service companies. This allowed the service companies to claim that the parts they used were equal to those of the original manufacturers. As a result the original manufacturers lost control over the lifetime performance of their product. An analogous situation might be farming out the design of ROM's by computer or machine tool manufacturers.

Product specific test equipment may be another worthwhile investment, if it is needed at this stage. Yet, it is often better to use generic test equipment that is usually lower in cost and more flexible and has a proportionately greater residual value than unique test equipment.

The Manager of Operations must agree with the CEO that investment will be deferred during the seed and start-up stage unless there is a compelling reason to allocate cash for investment purposes.

2. Keep the organization small.

Organization size can be kept to a minimum by farming out as much production work as possible during the seed and start-up stage. One or more production engineers will probably be required (unless consultants are hired) to complete the documentation and arrange for the preproduction run.

The preproduction run units also should be built using the same people, tooling and facilities as will be used for actual production. This requires that either the supplier is selected or that in-house manufacturing operations are established, prior to the preproduction run.

The selection of the production strategy will determine how rapidly employees must be added to the payroll. Conversely, the availability of trained employees may be a significant factor in determining how much work to farm out.

Section Five

People

Building a team.

During the seed and start-up stage the CEO's most important objective will be to build a team of excellent people and supporting organizations. This will consist of the initial employee team, the board of directors, investors, banker, consultants, and specialty suppliers. The need for consultants and specialty suppliers will depend on the marketing and production strategies that define the amount of work to be farmed out. Figure 5 depicts how the organization could look during the seed and start-up stage.

The entrepreneur turned CEO should give considerable thought to the capabilities and characteristics required of board members, needed to augment the shortcomings of the founders. If the product is a retail consumer item and doesn't involve engineering technologies, the company will be well advised to seek out venture capital organizations who have invested in similar items. If the product involves high technology, the converse would apply.

For example, having to explain the protocols and equipment requirements in sending and receiving over the same line in duplex communications, will be time consuming. Venture capital investors can learn very quickly due to their contact with many businesses. Unfortunately the natural resistance built into people who are not familiar with a technology can delay or prevent board approval of critical items.

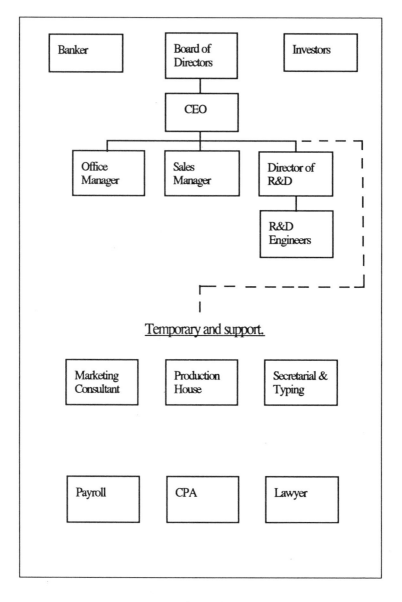

Figure 5

To a certain extent the composition of the board of directors will   be determined by the investors. The CEO will want board members experienced in markets, production and technologies closely related to the company's product. He should obtain a commitment from the venture capital firm on which member of the firm will sit on the board. It probably will be the partner who has taken the lead in negotiating the investment, but sometimes the firm appoints an associate to the board. This may or not be advantageous and should be agreed upon ahead of time.

Venture capital firms frequently bring another firm or two into the investment. This helps the lead investor spread his risk. It also gives him exposure to a wider range of potential investments when the other firms invite him to participate where they have taken the lead. The spreading of investments between venture capital firms may be good for the investors, but is not necessarily good for the company. Too many divergent views on the board can complicate the CEO's job. If one venture capital firm joins the investment based on another firms recommendation, it can be a stumbling block to raising additional funds later if it becomes disenchanted with the product.

Style and leadership are two qualities important to the success of a CEO. Style is a distinctly personal quality, unique to each CEO. Some styles are more effective than others under differing circumstances.

Leading by example, effective communications, and the ability to instill confidence in an organization are indisputable attributes of effective leadership. Although style and leadership are subjects best left to social scientists, the CEO will find that his ability to gain acceptance for policies and actions will depend on his style and leadership.

The following are examples of issues that can elicit a negative response from the organization and be troublesome for the CEO. Each is a legitimate objective from the perspective of the CEO.

(a) Constraints imposed by cash management can be perceived as being restrictive and negative, and not strategic or necessary.

(b) Keeping the organization focused on objectives can be viewed as narrow, and not as a strength that helps assure success.

(c) Messages such as "we cannot be all things to all people" can be viewed as non-responsive to customers rather than a strategic statement that keeps the company from over extending itself.

By communicating with those around him and explaining the reason behind his decisions, the CEO can reduce the potential for a negative response.

The CEO will find that his success can be dependent on how effectively he leads the company and the extent to which he gains the endorsement of the organization. Even in a turnaround situation where large numbers of employees are let go, the CEO must gain the support and confidence of the remaining employees if the company is to recover fully.

ACTIONS TO CONSIDER TAKING.

1. Select investors carefully.

Although there are thousands of entrepreneurs seeking funds from investors, the entrepreneur turned CEO should attempt to be selective in his choice of investors. Investors who are deluged with requests for money and with business plans from entrepreneurs, would appear to have the upper hand when negotiating with the entrepreneur.

The reverse can be the case when the entrepreneur has an excellent product or service concept and presents it well. There is a dearth of top grade investment opportunities and venture capital firms find themselves competing among themselves for an opportunity to invest in top grade ideas.

This is another reason to wait, if possible, until after the product has received customer acceptance before seeking funds from venture capital firms. The entrepreneur turned CEO who can prove he has a hot product or service idea, will develop interest from several venture capital firms. This will place the company in an advantageous negotiating position, where it can select the investors who are best for the company.

2. Take care when selecting the board of directors.

The investors will elect board members based on their agreement with the company when they make their investment.

There will be a tendency to fill the remaining seats with founders or family members. This may be important for voting purposes, but eliminates the potential for appointing board members who can make important contributions in areas where the CEO and founders lack inexperience.

3. Preselect your banker.

It is unlikely the company will require borrowings (or qualify for them from a bank) during the seed and start-up stage. Most businesses will require bank credit during the takeoff stage.

The CEO can enhance the company's ability to obtain the necessary credit if he has established good relationships with several bankers before the company needs the money. To accomplish this the business plan should be discussed with the bankers and the CEO should meet with the bankers regularly (perhaps monthly following board meetings) to discuss the company's progress. The likely nature of the loan agreement should be discussed, including the covenants and restrictions on which the bank may insist. This can help the company reach agreement with their bank of choice. The agreement should be entered into before funds will be required.

At the appropriate time the company can make known its cash requirements and, assuming the company meets the terms of the loan agreement, the funds should be forthcoming.

4. Begin your communications program, now.

During the seed and start-up stage the company will be small and the CEO can, for the most part, communicate informally with his organization. It is still a good idea to begin a formal communications program during this stage. Once started, the communications program will become part of the company's culture, involving the CEO in a positive role.

Initially the small group of employees and founders can meet after the board meeting (but at least monthly) for a briefing by the CEO and for an open discussion of issues and events.

This is an opportunity to begin building a team. The CEO should give special attention to how he wants to conduct these meetings. He should keep in mind that they also provide him with an opportunity to exert his style and influence on the company's culture.

5. Hire the best.

When the decision is made to fill a position the CEO should make certain the company hires the best. It is frequently better to leave a position unfilled than to hire someone in whom the CEO is not completely satisfied.

6. Keep control over salaries.

Employees are usually hired at this stage in the company's development without the benefit of a formal salary structure that provides guidelines for the worth of each position. The salary issue confronts the CEO, who is attempting to hire the best, every time the company hires a new employee. Each hiring situation seems more important than those preceding it, with each new prospective employee viewed as preeminently qualified. The tendency will be for each successive salary offer to be higher than the preceding offer. Eventually the first "outstanding" person will be receiving a lower salary than the person hired last. It is absolutely certain that salary information will become common knowledge, and unjustified disparities will haunt the CEO.

The CEO should think about how he will want to administer employee compensation as the company grows. At some point he will want to establish a compensation plan for the company. The board of directors will expect the CEO to present them with a compensation plan for their approval, especially in as far as the plan relates to stock options.

Meanwhile the CEO should keep personal control over salaries (and stock options if not controlled by the board), including salary increases. He also should retain final approval for hiring all employees, including the nature of the offer. Establishing this policy now assures control over the quality and size of the organization and provides a framework for delegating hiring authority later.

Moving and relocation expenses also should be controlled by the CEO until the company adopts a formal policy. Although each move will differ, there should be a consistent basis for determining reimbursements.

Building an outstanding team and rewarding people for outstanding performance is an area of personal satisfaction for the CEO. Managing the performance - compensation relationship can, however, be a land mine in the path of success.

> Cash during the early stages of a new company is the CEO's most precious asset. It is hard to raise, and easy to spend.

PART TWO

THE TAKEOFF STAGE

Lift off.

Just as an airplane lifts tentatively off the ground in the first moments of flight, the start-up company receives an influx of initial orders thrusting it into the takeoff stage. At first the volume is low and steady, but then climbs at an rapid rate.

The takeoff stage is, in many ways, a period of transition, with the company moving from a small team working feverishly to launch the product and gain initial customer acceptance, to a progressively larger organization, broadening its customer base and improving its ability to produce and deliver product.

There also is an early period in the takeoff stage where cash flow is negative and volume is so low that market share is hardly noticeable. It is followed by a period where cash flow normally turns positive and market share catches the serious attention of competitors.

A new kind of person will start to be added to the organization during the takeoff stage. These people will include functional experts (such as in accounting, sales, and purchasing) who will tend to make decisions using functional criteria. The use of economic ordering points (E.O.P.) by purchasing is an example.

The CEO will find it increasingly difficult to have employees focus on company objectives and not on functional goals. Because the organization remains somewhat small during the takeoff stage, it is still possible for the CEO to relate individually to people and to directly influence their actions. The CEO's areas of responsibility remain the same: Cash, Strategy, Marketing, Operations and People.

Section One

Cash

The Chief Financial Officer.

During the takeoff stage emphasis will be placed on expense control and implementation of accounting systems. It is important to remember that the company remains in jeopardy until cash flow turns positive. Without positive cash flow the company will need a continuing infusion of new money. Yet, there is a practical limit on how much the company can borrow or secure through equity financing. The slightest set back in sales or direct costs, can throw the company into a tailspin from which it may not recover.

An important question will be when to hire a Chief Financial Officer (CFO). There is a possibility the arrangements made for handling accounting matters during the start-up stage will be adequate during the early period of the takeoff stage, while cash flow is negative. An experienced financial manager should be in place to assure control when the dollar value of inventories, purchases, receivables or other assets become significant.

The presence of a CFO is also important for the development and implementation of systems. The CFO should be highly qualified in determining which systems are needed and in how they should be acquired and installed. He should quickly establish a plan for installing accounting systems. The CFO should prepare improved projections of cash needs and provide the CEO with good advice on the use of cash.

ACTIONS TO CONSIDER TAKING.

1. Establish crucial accounting systems.

The company will not survive unless accounting systems are in place that, (a) give the CEO and his management team, timely and effective financial information on the status of the business, and (b) provide for control.

From the perspective of the CEO there are two categories of systems: accounting and operating. Many fully developed systems combine the two in a single system. The complexity and expense of developing an integrated system make such a development an unrealistic task during the takeoff stage.

A better approach is to identify which systems are most important and to install them first. To the extent it is important, the individual systems can be developed to fit into an integrated system later.

Systems can be an extremely expensive and time consuming undertaking and should not be thought of lightly. The CEO's objective is to put systems in place immediately for critical areas, and to do it as inexpensively as possible.

Attempting to develop a system that integrates accounting and operating activities is probably a mistake for two reasons. First, operating management doesn't know its needs at this stage in the company's development. Second, the development of such a system can be a black hole into which considerable amounts of cash can be thrown.

Another aspect of systems that deserves the attention of the CEO, are the types of reports generated by the system. The reports should supply the information required by management to run the business and should highlight information to be brought to managements attention. Reports should require a minimum time to read.

Receivables, for example, should be shown on the monthly operating statement so that management can quickly see the amount they have changed and whether they require immediate management attention. An effective receivables report, to which management will turn to next, will show receivables by their age. An effective receivables report will show receivables that are less than 60 days old, followed by those that are 60 to 90 days old, 90 to 180 days old, and then those that are over 180 days old, and list by customer name those that are over 90 days old or are over a specified dollar amount no matter what their age.

The CEO may only be interested in the aging report, but the Marketing VP should want to know the names of delinquent customers. This will allow him to identify why the customer hasn't paid the invoice. To be effective the system must be capable of generating the types of reports needed by management.

There are system packages available on the market that may meet the company's requirements and should be investigated before spending money on developing new systems. Computerized accounting, Manufacturing Resource Planning (MRP), and service dispatch systems, for example, are available on the open market.

The first systems that probably should be installed are:

1. General accounting.

2. Inventory control.

3. Production control.

4. Budgets.

The general accounting system should produce, (a) a statement of operating accounts that can be balanced monthly, (b) a monthly operating statement, (c) a monthly balance sheet, and (d) a monthly receivable report.

The inventory control report should provide a monthly status of the cash tied up in inventory and the quantities of each item included in the inventory.

Finished goods, work in process and raw materials are the three major categories of inventory for a manufacturing company. A product service company may require inventory reports on parts, supplies, and materials used in its service business. A retail store may require an inventory of stock on hand.

The CEO needs to know the amount of cash tied up in inventory, how many additional dollars will be tied up in inventory as sales grow, and whether there is any inventory that is not moving. He will need to be certain that Marketing knows what units are available for shipment so that realistic shipping promises can be given to customers, and that Operations knows the status of raw and in process inventory.

The production control system for a company that initially farms out its production will merely be a system tracking units on order, shipping promises and deliveries. If the company manufactures the product in house the production control system will cover all aspects of production, including ordering of materials, factory releases, dispatching and tracking of work in process. The starting point for any production control system will be the bill of materials, which is one reason the documentation from engineering must be accurate and complete. The initial production control system need not cover all aspects of a total MRP system, but could be based on pertinent portions of commercially available MRP programs.

Service businesses may require a different type of control system. The system for a product service company performing service at the customers site and at the company's service center, will be keyed to the dispatching of its service technicians. Initially a stand alone system for inventory kept at the service center and in each technician's vehicle can provide a minimum level of inventory control, with technicians reporting their inventory usage each day as they exchange defective parts for good ones. An ideal system would identify all equipment under contract, identify the equipment (by type and manufacturer) each technician has been trained to service, and identify the equipment for which each technician carries parts. Such a system must retain several variables in memory.

(a) A list of good parts carried by each technician in his vehicle.

(b) A list of the equipment (by type and manufacturer) on which the technician has been trained.

(c) A list of the equipment installed at the customers site.

(d) The location of every technician in the service territory.

For management purposes, the system also should be able to retain in memory the amount of time required to complete each service call and the amount of time required to travel from one service call to the next.

Finally a system of budgets and measurements needs to be established, with accounts established for each category of expense.

The CEO plays an important role by assuring that these four systems (general accounting, inventory control, production control and budgets) are capable of meeting the simpler needs of the company during the takeoff stage, and of being easily adapted to a larger organization as the company grows.

2. Use procedures to communicate priorities.

Procedures are a form of communication that should be used by the CEO to define how he wants to conduct high priority activities. During the takeoff stage the CEO should decide those areas that should be covered by procedures, and when and how to install the procedures. (Procedures for controlling investment and expense should have been established during the seed and start-up stage.)

Entrepreneurs turned CEO may be hesitant to adopt procedures as they are frequently viewed as restrictive and bureaucratic. This aversion to bureaucracy is healthy. The last thing the CEO wants is for the company to become paralyzed by procedures and policies, or paralyzed from adhering too strictly to organization channels. It must be kept in mind, however, that the company will require structure (including procedures) if it is to function effectively as it grows.

The issue isn't whether to have procedures, but how many procedures and how flexible the structure should be.

During the seed and start-up stage a procedure should have been established requiring the CEO to approve most commitments before expenditures are made. The CEO will want to begin delegating this authority during the takeoff stage. If authority is to be delegated, it will be necessary to add a new element of control; namely budgets.

Initially budgets can be kept simple. The investment budget can remain at the corporate level until later. The expense budget can be allocated among the various functions, with budgets established for each function. The number of accounts can initially be kept to a minimum and be increased as the need dictates. As the company grows, expense budgets can be established by each function for their subfunctions.

One purpose of an expense budget is to permit the CEO (and the rest of the management team) to analyze how the company is spending its money and to identify problems. The system should provide timely (monthly, a few days after the books are closed) and useful information, such as reports identifying variances from budget and, as appropriate, from prior accounting periods.

The CEO also should keep in mind that he loses a certain degree of control when he delegates approval to spend money and that the budget system only reports money that has been spent. Commitments obligating the company to spend money could have been made, without managements knowledge. These obligations will not appear on the monthly expense report.

A development contract where the company will pay the supplier when the work is completed will not appear on the financial statement when the contract is signed, but could severely impact earnings in a future quarter. When commitments are large, a mechanism must be adopted in the budget and reporting system that recognizes the impact of these commitments on future expenses. Accounting must be certain to recognize that commitments are a threat to the budget process and to the control of expenses.

Consistency in earnings becomes more important after the company goes public. A sudden change in earnings can receive unfavorable comment from financial analysts and negatively impact the company's stock price. Inconsistent monthly earnings also may deter investors before the company goes public, since erratic results can be an indication of poor management.

Three additional procedures should be incorporated as part of financial controls, (a) inventory levels, (b) receivables, (c) payables.

To a certain extent, establishing an approved inventory level can be accomplished through the budget process. Budgets tend to be static and are not sufficiently flexible for managing inventories, especially while the company is young and systems are not completely in place. From the CEO's perspective, controlling inventory requires three actions.

First, on at least a monthly basis, the CEO should approve the level of finished goods inventory for the following month, and establish the corresponding production level (or level of purchases if the product is purchased).

Second, the CEO should retain authority for approving all locations at which inventory will be kept.

Third, a system must be in place that will permit monitoring the first two actions.

Without control (spelled with capital letters) over inventory the CEO cannot manage cash flow, and if he cannot manage cash flow he risks everything.

The receivable reports mentioned earlier, should permit effective management of receivables. The CEO should receive and monitor these reports, and remain responsible for deciding whether customer accounts are closed (C.O.D. only) or whether legal or collection actions are to be taken.

Runaway receivables are another way to court disaster.

Payables should be stretched as long as reasonable (perhaps 90 days), while also maintaining an excellent credit rating, the goodwill of suppliers and avoiding interest payments. This should be the responsibility of the CFO, but the CEO should routinely follow up on the status of payables. Payables represent a type of borrowing and it's wise to retain good relations with major suppliers.

3. Define cash requirements for growth.

During the takeoff stage one of the primary concerns of the CEO is to be certain the company can handle growth. An important aspect of being able to handle growth, is having the cash available with which to fund growth.

Cash requirements for people, inventories and receivables must be forecast with some degree of accuracy. Cash flow projections at different growth rates can help establish cash requirements.

With cash flow projections in hand, and with knowledge of how the product is being received in the marketplace, the

CEO can make judgements concerning the company's strategy; depending on his, and the boards, vision for the company.

If the company is to remain closely held, growth will be limited by the ability of the company to generate cash internally coupled with its ability to obtain additional investment from the original investors or to borrow money from the bank. Local service companies or companies serving a small niche market, may consider adopting such an approach.

If the vision for the company is for it to become as large as it can, additional financing may be required. An initial public offering or the issuance of bonds are two ways to obtain cash for growth.

The CEO, in conjunction with the board, will need to decide when the company should initiate a public offering. The company also will need to decide whether it should wait until it can issue stock using NASDQ or issue it sooner through an exchange such as Vancouver or Denver. The CEO should strive to use the approach that generates the most cash for the company over the long term. There may be a stigma associated with some exchanges other than NASDQ, which the CEO should investigate. Advice should be obtained from an investment banker before making any decisions with respect to an initial public offering.

The company also may formulate a less traditional strategy for raising money, such as establishing foreign companies who have access to local capital.

A good CEO also will make certain that the company is ready to go public and thereby offer the public a sound investment.

4. Avoid consigning inventory.

Consigning inventory is frequently the worst idea that marketing or sales can propose. Occasionally a competitive situation mandates consignment, such as when the practice is so ingrained in the industry that it cannot be avoided. The need to consign inventory often represents a failure on the part of marketing or sales.

If, for example, inventory is consigned to a distributor, (see appendix) the distributor has little motivation to sell the product, other than the markup he receives. Distributors will attempt to have companies consign inventory when the product is new and market acceptance has not yet been established. The last thing a new company wants is for the product to sit on the distributor's shelf tying up inventory dollars. The company wants the distributor to be committed to selling the product.

An example of how consignment of inventory can work to the disadvantage of the company is one that occurred at a start-up company manufacturing a new lighting product. The Marketing VP sold the product to a large distributor in the southeast but gave the distributor a letter committing to repurchase the inventory if it did not sell. After several months the distributor returned the material (at the company's expense) and the company had to refund the sales price. The distributor had made little effort to sell the product claiming that the Marketing VP had committed to have the company's direct sales force sell the product. When the start-up company's product was originally sold to the distributor in the southeast, it created an illusion of sales that impressed the board. The sales, in fact, did not exist.

If a potential customer requests consignment there may be a valid reason for proceeding with the arrangement. An example might be where a customer commits to using the product but is unable to forecast usage and doesn't want to work through a distributor. By having the product on hand the customer can draw from the consigned inventory as the product is needed. This arrangement worked well for a business using large quantities of hardware, where the supplier replenished stock as it was used.

The fact remains that consigned inventory represents another location for which the company must account. Consigning inventory to a customer is another form of price cutting.

An alternative to consignment (especially for larger or higher priced items) could be rental, if the customer wants to evaluate the product before purchasing it.

5. Keep the lid on expenses.

As the organization grows and sales effort expands, there will be a tendency to spend money on nonessentials. It is sometimes difficult to distinguish between brilliant marketing and extravagance but the CEO needs to be certain that enthusiasm doesn't override good judgement.

Section Two

Strategy

Position the company for future growth.

The takeoff stage should be used to position the company for growth. Actual performance of the product and company should be compared with the performance projected by the original business plan.

The reexamination should result in a corporate growth strategy, which will have the benefit of actual operating experience during the start-up and takeoff stages. Successful growth will depend on the company having put in place (or made provision for) a series of essential actions. Part three, the Growth Stage covers these actions. Depending on the company's progress the CEO could begin implementing these actions now.

The company should not undertake a new strategic direction while it is in a negative cash flow position. Unless the original business plan has turned out to be completely invalid, decisions will continue to be more tactical than strategic, and represent adjustments to the original plan, focused on the near term.

ACTIONS TO CONSIDER TAKING.

1. Say no to activities that diffuse focus.

A major trap during the takeoff stage is for the company to begin broadening its market or product too rapidly. When the company is doing well there will be a certain amount of euphoria that can lead management to believe that they will be successful at everything they attempt. Enthusiasm is commendable but, actions should be constrained while the company has limited resources. Resources still need to be focused on actions that will advance the company toward its primary objective.

Pressures will build to enhance, or otherwise change, the product or service. Customers will request additional features (styles, service etc.): Prospective customers will request that products or services be sold in areas where the company is not yet ready to provide the needed customer service or support: New distributors and manufacturer representatives will request to carry your product or represent your company.

Unless a request dovetails into existing plans, or unless it represents a strategic breakthrough, the company will need to resist the temptation the request represents. The CEO needs to know of these requests and help the organization say no.

It is frequently difficult to say no and still maintain enthusiasm within an organization, but it is something the CEO will need to learn how to do. It's helpful to keep from saying no any more than necessary, such as when the request doesn't adversely affect the use of resources. It's also important to discuss with the organization why it's necessary to say no. Retaining all requests on file, so that they may be examined while formulating the company's growth strategy, can help curtail negative feelings, and also contribute toward the development of the growth strategy.

The organization should be reminded that adding a feature or service can have an inordinate impact on the use of resources. A simple new feature, for example, requires engineering to change drawings, add parts or change configurations and to verify that quality will not suffer because of the change. The additional parts result in increased inventory and possibly new tooling. Finished product inventory also will increase to accommodate the wider product offering, (unless it is kept solely as a special for a particular customer, which raises the question as to the need for the new feature). Increased parts inventory for servicing the product also may be required, as will changes to the service manual.

If a prospective customer, remote from areas where the product is currently sold, wants to buy the product, the company should consider the impact of the remote sale on distribution and service. A single sale to a remote customer can be handled on an exception or trial basis, making the customer aware of probable delays in service or delivery.

One example of where remote sales could have hurt a company, was where the CEO of a company barely in the takeoff stage, began investigating export opportunities to Europe and the Middle East. The problems of how to distribute, support or service the product, or what type of warranty to provide, or the availability of hard currency (in Egypt) weren't being considered.

2. Know how your customers see you.

An important reason for keeping customer requests for product and service changes on file, is that they can provide important insights into market opportunities or product shortcomings. They are also helpful in developing a product plan as part of the company's strategic plan.

Knowing how the product is performing is critical to the development of a growth strategy. Records of warranty claims is one source for this information. Equally important is determining how customers' perceive the product to be performing. Customer perceptions can be discerned if the company's quality plan investigates problems that go beyond warranty claims. A customer survey also can be a powerful adjunct to a quality control plan; especially for a service company where perceptions are vital.

A service company can send questionnaires on a quarterly or semiannual basis, to its customers to ask about their satisfaction with the service and about specific performance criteria. The questionnaire should be sent to two or three levels in the organization. It can be used with a telephone survey, either to follow-up on complaints or problems uncovered by the questionnaire or as an adjunct to the written survey.

An example of the importance of such a survey is a company whose own records showed nearly spotless performance in meeting its response time guarantee with a particular customer. This customer was dissatisfied with the promptness of service it received, though the technician had always reached the site within the prescribed time limit. The technician had made it a practice to go directly to the equipment room to work on the problem. After the survey disclosed that the customer was not aware of the technicians on time arrival, he made it a point to report to the person responsible for the equipment. From that point forward the customer was satisfied, though the actual response time had remained unchanged.

A side benefit of a customer satisfaction survey is that it helps keep mailing lists up to date, which can be important to marketing and sales.

The CEO must be certain that customer perceptions about the product or service, are consistent with the assumptions contained in the original business plan.

A start-up company introduced a new pudding of Dutch origins, to the San Francisco market. The company used very appealing advertising, depicting an attractive Dutch girl changing from wooden shoes to modern dress, eating this delightfully modern pudding, to elicit interest in the product.

Although initial sales were good, repeat sales were initially somewhat disappointing. The carton containing the pudding was similar to a milk container and was very difficult to open. The glue kept the spout firmly closed requiring the user to tear the package apart to get to the pudding. Investors and friends of the CEO were among the first to buy the product, so that the CEO received immediate and vocal feedback. The customers' perceptions were that the pudding was excellent, but that it wasn't worth the trouble and mess associated with opening the carton.

Section Three

Marketing

Pricing, and its links to value, cost and volume.

During the takeoff stage, marketing emphasis will continue to be on the building of constituencies while establishing a reputation for excellent quality and service. Excitement can be created for the product or service as first one, then another, and then another constituency expresses satisfaction with the product or service. It is important for marketing to create excitement and not expect customers to automatically flock to the product, because its technology is so good or the product so unique.

The company also needs to establish a pricing strategy, either early in the takeoff stage or, if possible, during the start-up stage. The CEO should retain final authority over the company's pricing policy with an approval procedure included in the pricing policy, delineating approval requirements for various pricing actions.

The pricing strategy should consider the conditions that will exist during three stages in the company's growth.

1. Takeoff stage.

2. Growth stage.

3. Maturing stage.

Figure 6 depicts these stages. The grid superimposed on each stage is shown in figure 7. The grid depicts the impact of volume on costs along the horizontal axis, and the uniqueness or worth of the product to the customer along the vertical axis.

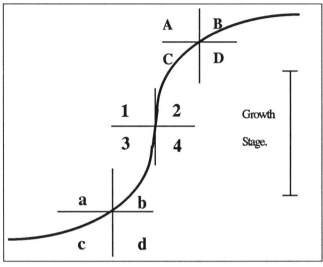

Figure 6

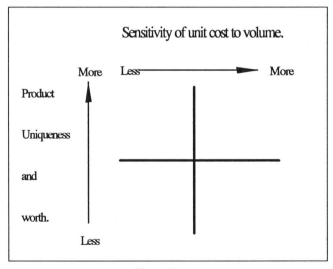

Figure 7

Learning curve theory was initially used with great success during the second world war to project schedules and costs. (See appendix.) Learning curve theory says that costs will decrease on a predictable basis every time volume doubles. Figure 8 shows a 90% learning curve with the anticipated reduction in man-hours. Some products have a 90% learning curve, others an 80% curve and others different curves still. Services can have learning curves of 95% and higher, indicating that volume, by itself, won't result in significantly lower costs or in cost leadership.

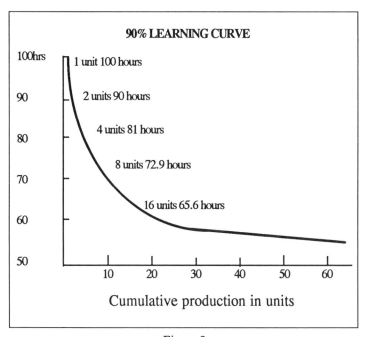

Figure 8

The Boston Consulting Group took this well documented theory and applied it to corporate strategy by equating volume to market share. The company with the highest market share will have more sales each year than its competitors, and will therefore have greater volume and achieve cost leadership. Market share, under this concept, becomes a key corporate objective since it results, by definition, in cost leadership.

It should be kept in mind that a cost leadership position can still be challenged if a competitor takes advantage of the industries' total experience and reenters the learning curve at a point close to where the leading company is currently operating. Competitors who are willing to invest in the latest equipment and technology can thereby challenge the current market leader. The Japanese, for example, didn't start making automobiles in the late 1940's based on the know how of the thirties. Instead, they ascertained the current state of the art, took advantage of the cumulative industry experience, improved on it and achieved cost leadership.

Referring to the grid in figure 7, a product whose cost is very sensitive to volume would be positioned to the right side of the grid. A service whose costs are insensitive to volume would be placed on the left side of the grid.

Product uniqueness, and the competitive advantage inherent therein, is depicted on the vertical axis. The greater the value of the product to the customer or the more unique the product and the more barriers to entry, the higher on the vertical axis the product or service would be positioned. For example, overnight delivery of packages and letters has greater value to the customer than does ordinary mail.

With respect to the growth curve, figure 6, the greatest period of price elasticity occurs during the growth stage of the product (or for a single product new company, the company itself). The growth stage, therefore, represents the period during which price has the greatest impact on market size and, possibly, on market share.

One reason the growth stage can impact market share is that competitors may not recognize they are losing market position. In a growing market, competitors' sales can remain constant or grow at a slow rate, hiding a deteriorating market position from its management. Management may not recognize a market share problem if they aren't losing customers, losing sales or having to reduce their work force. Even alert competitors or competitors whose industry trade group reports on sales by its members, may not pay much attention to a new company until the new company's sales are significant.

This is one of several reasons why it may not be to the advantage of a new company to belong to an industry trade group.

Set your pricing strategy.

The starting point for arriving at a pricing strategy is to assess, (1) how unique the product or service is and how much value it has to customers over competing products or technologies, and (2) to determine to what extent volume will impact costs.

The assessment will indicate in which quadrant of the grid, figure 9, the product or service is to be positioned; which, in turn, suggests the appropriate pricing strategy for the growth stage. A pricing strategy involving higher prices and greater margins may be best for the company when an extremely unique product or service has great value to the customer, and if volume (and therefore market share) doesn't result in significantly lower costs (quadrant #1).

Such a strategy can generate cash that has intrinsic strategic value, helping to fund growth and eventually acquisitions.

A service company serving a single geographic area probably won't have its unit costs reduced by higher volume (assuming a minimum density of items serviced is achieved). A value pricing strategy that generates cash can provide the company with the cash it needs to expand geographically (to another part of the country or world).

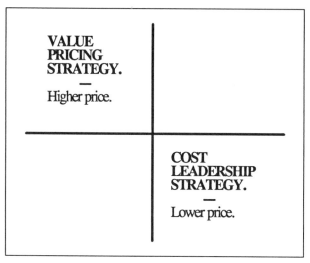

Figure 9

If the product is not unique and if costs can be significantly reduced with higher volume, a cost leadership pricing strategy (quadrant #4) could be adopted. With this strategy the company attempts to capture a commanding market share, resulting in higher volume and lower costs than competitors. With such a strategy the company with cost leadership has pricing leadership, since competitors will hesitate to lower their prices for fear of retaliation.

The company adopting a value pricing strategy (quadrant #1) may have some influence on market growth, through an even higher price. This would require a virtual monopoly, or where prestige or other value creates an implied monopoly. The danger of using such a tactic is that it can result in a price umbrella, encouraging new competitors with alternative technologies as replacements for the company's product or service.

Once the CEO has selected the most effective pricing strategy for the growth stage, he should examine whether conditions during the takeoff stage fit the same strategy. He should look at current and projected costs, and at the prices of competing products or technologies.

If current total costs (including overhead) are higher than the price of competing products, the company may be forced into a value pricing strategy (quadrant "a") during the takeoff stage. This should not represent a major problem if the product or service has value to the customer, which it should have or the product should have been seriously questioned earlier. If costs are projected to fall rapidly, the company could initially accept a lower price (with some losses) anticipating that it will have cost leadership in the very near future. This course of action should be carefully scrutinized since it aggravates the company's negative cash flow position. There is also a strong possibility that the company's product will be in short supply during the takeoff stage and possibly into the growth stage. A value pricing strategy makes good sense while the product is in short supply.

Another factor to consider in arriving at a pricing strategy is the cost of sales and distribution. If significant savings can be realized through large orders, volume discounts should be considered. FTC and antitrust guidelines should be followed when establishing lower prices based on volume.

The CEO should be careful not to establish prices and discount schedules for the takeoff stage, which will undermine or invalidate the pricing strategy planned for the growth stage.

Establishing low prices during the start-up or takeoff stages to capture important initial orders, can play havoc with a value pricing strategy later. Raising prices more than 10 to 20% can result in a reputation for price gouging with resultant ill will and sales resistance. It is much better to establish a list price near the price intended for the value pricing strategy (or whatever the ultimate strategy is to be) and to discount from it.

All proposals and invoices should clearly show the list price with the discount. It is even better when a reason can be established for the one time discount, and for the reason to be clearly stated in the proposal and invoice. For example:

"We are pleased to quote 50 of our revolutionary new widgets (R.N.W.'s) at $500 each, and a total price of $25,000.

Since your company will be evaluating the R.N.W's and will incur costs to complete the evaluation, we will help offset those costs by reducing our price by 50%, resulting in a discounted price of $25 each. The total net price to you will, therefore, be $12,500."

A product service business will confront additional problems in formulating and executing its pricing strategy. In this type of business the "product" changes with each service transaction. A service technician for a computer service company can expect to find different problems at each customer location. At the first location, perhaps the mother board has failed: At the second location, the CRT may have failed: At the third location the problem may have been with the key board: At the fourth location the unit may merely have required an adjustment.

Each call will require a different amount of time to complete: Each call will require a different level of experience and training on the part of the technician: Each call will require the use of more or less expensive test equipment: Each call will require the use of spare parts ranging in value from a few dollars to thousands of dollars. It is very likely that service calls involving identical components (for example the motherboard) will require different lengths of time to complete. The motherboard at each location can have a different problem.

Two people pricing the same transaction can arrive at different prices depending on how they treat the various elements of the service call. For example, travel time could be averaged between all calls for the day, be established as a standard based on one years experience, be the actual time taken to reach the customers site, or be based on another standard such as an average travel time from the company's service depot. If actual travel time is used the customer can receive widely varying invoices for identical service calls. The location from where the technician began his travel will vary and the amount of traffic (especially in metropolitan areas) will vary depending on the time of day. Time spent at the customers site also can vary when serving identical equipment, having identical problems. At one location the equipment is located in an office building readily accessible to the technician. At the next site the equipment is located within a complex of buildings, requiring the technician to go through the main gate and obtain a gate pass.

Preparing a quotation is even more difficult than preparing an invoice. All the facts concerning the service call are known when the invoice is prepared, while a quotation is based on estimates where many facts may not be known.

For these types of service businesses, pricing guidelines must be established to help assure pricing consistency and to incorporate predetermined margins in the price. With pricing guidelines, an appropriate pricing strategy can be developed for the service business or different strategies can be developed for different segments of the service business.

Distributors, who are service companies, will probably not find it appropriate to adopt a cost leadership pricing strategy. The manufacturer has control over costs and can use the learning curve to predict lower costs as volume increases. Only those distributors who can significantly lower distribution costs, such as with automated warehousing, will be able to relate the learning curve to volume. Most distributors will not be able achieve a learning curve that will significantly affect their costs and should not, therefore, consider a price leadership strategy.

Pricing is not a science. Pricing is an art that has a direct bearing on the growth and profitability of a company. Therefore the CEO will want to approve the pricing strategy and establish a procedure for delegating pricing authority, indicating when his approval is required.

This procedure will be different for a company whose average transaction size is $500 with sales of $10 million, from that of another $10 million company whose average transaction size is $700,000. In one instance there will be 20,000 transactions a year, in the other only 14 or 15 transactions during the same period.

In the former instance, the authority to cut price up to 10% for transactions under $1000 might be delegated to a local manager. Larger discounts or discounts on larger orders (up to specified amounts) might be delegated to the Marketing VP. Authority for even higher discounts or discounts on even larger quantities and to change the price list, would be retained by the CEO.

In the second instance the CEO probably will want to approve every price until the company gets substantially larger. He can then establish guidelines within which smaller jobs can be priced by the Marketing VP, while retaining authority to approve prices for large or unusual jobs.

Another aspect of pricing in which the CEO should initially be involved, is the size of distributor discounts and representatives commissions. The larger the discount the more room there is for the distributor to cut the price to the user, which can result in the company losing control over pricing. At issue, is whether pricing control achieved through smaller discounts is more important than the additional distributor support that might be achieved through larger discounts.

With respect to commissions paid to representatives, the larger the commission the greater the opportunity for the representative to use a portion of his commission for kickbacks. Since kickbacks are illegal throughout most of the world it is wise to keep commissions as low as possible. The CEO should decide the size of sales representatives commissions.

The affect of discounts and commissions on multiple sales channels (distributors, representatives, and direct) also should be considered when establishing discounts and commissions.

Besides establishing a pricing strategy and pricing procedures, the CEO should consider the following actions during the takeoff stage.

ACTIONS TO CONSIDER TAKING.

1. Follow up on every sale.

It is extremely important to assure that the product is functioning to the complete satisfaction of customers. Feedback should be obtained on the following questions.

1. Were there premature failures? If so, how many were there and what was the cause of failure?

2. Were any problems experienced during installation of the product? If so, what were they and how can they be corrected?

3. Were the customers' expectations fully met? If not, why not?

For a service business the questions also could include:

1. Was response to the customers' call within the specified response time?

2. Was the service performed in the time specified?

3. Were there any failures after the initial service call, or were repeat service calls required to restore the equipment to satisfactory operation? If repeat calls were necessary, why?

During the takeoff stage the CEO should allocate sufficient resources to obtain answers to these types of questions, and be certain he knows the results of the fact finding efforts.

The best time to find out about premature failures or installation problems as well as about other important problems, is before a great deal of product has been shipped. If the CEO doesn't make it his business to find out about these problems when they first arise, he is likely to find out about them after much damage has been done to the company. Most people don't like bringing bad news to the boss and will sometimes delay informing him, hoping the problem won't be serious and will resolve itself.

2. Establish sales budgets, now.

The CEO should participate in establishing sales budgets during the takeoff stage, and assure himself that sales budgets have been established for each salesman, account and territory.

It is essential for the CEO to have a good grasp on the reality of the sales forecast. It is the basis for a wide range of decisions concerning cash requirements, staffing, investments and production schedules, and should be accurate.

An orders budget also should be established for products or services requiring a long lead time between order placement and delivery. With long lead times, sales can be forecast with reasonable certainty as can production and cash requirements.

Products having short lead times can be subject to violent swings in demand. Large swings in demand such as with seasonal products can require a build up of finished goods inventory to level production. Such an inventory buildup uses cash and raises the specter of obsolete inventory. The accuracy of the sales forecast is extremely important.

There also should be assurance that the sales or order budgets represent a sound basis for measuring the performance of salesmen and sales management. This is especially important if salesmen and sales managers are on a commission plan.

Budgets by account or territory will permit an analysis of sales variances (good or bad) and establish a means for targeting customers and concentrating resources.

3. Promotion without advertising.

Development of constituencies (see figure 4, page 55) can provide the basis for inexpensive sales promotion. Advertising can be very costly and represent a major cash commitment, and probably should be deferred until the growth stage by taking advantage of a well structured publicity campaign.

New products or services will nearly always receive space in a trade or business publication. Articles can frequently be published that discuss the benefits of the product or service. An article written by the customer who tested your product, or by an editor or reporter of a trade or business publication, has the added advantage of believability. An advertisement on the other hand can easily be dismissed as biased and self serving (which it is). Industry meetings and shows afford another opportunity for reaching potential customers, although many of these shows have become very costly.

The press treats initial product announcements as news. Product announcements should be the first step in any publicity campaign. When advertising has appeared or articles have been published about the product, the product loses its news worthiness and the company loses its opportunity for free publicity.

A logical sequence of events for a publicity campaign would include:

(a) Press tour announcing the introduction of the new product or service, including interviews with magazine, newspaper, radio and television editors and reporters.

(b) News releases sent to all editors who were not reached during the press tour. The news releases and press tour should be coordinated to assure that each editor receives the information in time to meet the deadline for publication in his next issue.

(c) Work with editors to place articles prepared by the company, or preferably, written by customers, consultants or other third parties.

(d) Use direct mail to reach targeted customers. Previously prepared news releases or articles can be used as direct mail pieces.

(e) Telemarketing can be used to reach targeted customers, screen prospects, follow up on direct mail and schedule sales calls (for company or distributor salesmen, or manufacturer representatives).

(f) Arrange for insertion of bingo cards or other mailers in new product sections of trade publications.

(g) Exhibit at, or attend industry shows.

(h) Prepare and distribute, as appropriate, point of sale displays.

(i) Prepare brochures, catalogs, posters, samples and other publicity material as appropriate.

(j) Consider space advertising for consumer products or other situations where name recognition and a broad audience favor advertising. Also when advertising can create relevant awareness, and possibly, demand for the product. Relevant awareness implies that the advertising will reach the proper audience.

Continue to avoid consigning inventory while promoting the product. Besides the reasons given earlier, the product probably will be in short supply during the takeoff stage and it is not wise to tie up inventory in consignment that could otherwise be sold.

4. Keep control over contract documents.

The CEO should continue to retain authority for approving changes to contractual documents during the takeoff stage.

Section Four

Operations

During the takeoff stage operating emphasis will be on quality and on meeting delivery commitments. A foundation must also be established for reducing product cost, or in the case of service, the cost of delivering the service. This can be done by developing a production plan that becomes part of the strategic plan.

An important strategic operating issue for a manufacturing company, is the level of contributed value. The extent to which manufacture of the product is performed by the company versus the amount of work that is farmed out, determines the level of contributed value. The more work done in house, or the greater the vertical integration the higher will be the contributed value.

Preparing for full production.

During the takeoff stage operations should formulate its recommendations for the production plan. Experience gained while meeting demand during the takeoff stage will help in the formulation of this plan.

Figure 10 depicts the process for developing the production plan for a product company. The process for developing a service delivery plan for a service company is very similar except for the following few items. (1) Franchise fees represent an additional capital resource. (2) Greater attention must be paid to manpower and training. (3) Engineering rather than manufacturing resources should be evaluated.

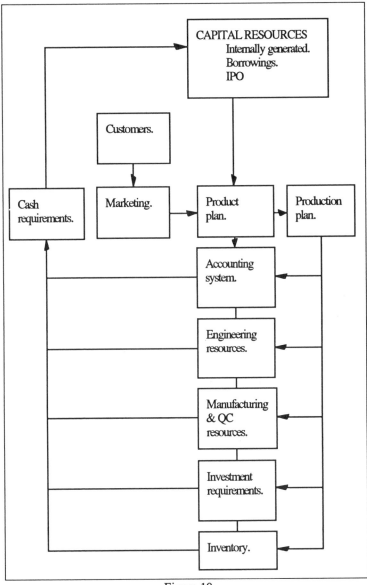

Figure 10

Operations will develop its plan based on the product plan or service offering, and on the volume forecast. The resulting production or service delivery plan defines the resource requirements. These requirements are compared with the availability of cash or people, which invariably leads to several iterations of the production or service delivery plan.

The CEO should initiate the process by establishing an initial estimate of available financial resources and by approving the production or service delivery plan and the volume forecast. A five year planning period is usually appropriate.

The greater the level of contributed value, the greater will be the allocation of resources to the production process. A plan that calls for a high level of contributed value probably will not have every aspect of the plan implemented simultaneously. Resource constraints, either cash or people, will dictate that the various elements of the plan be phased in over a period of time. In all likelihood this will be the first major program undertaken by the company and the CEO should assure himself that the plan is thoroughly prepared and documented.

The plan should cover the following elements.

1. Capital requirements.
   (a) Plant.
   (b) Facilities.
   (c) Equipment.

2. Organization structure.
   (a) Manufacturing and engineering integration.
   (b) Plant and direct labor management.
   (c) Manufacturing engineering.
   (d) Materials management.
   (e) Quality control.

3. Direct costs.
   (a) Labor (number, skills, levels and rates).
   (b) Materials.

4. Expense.
   (a) Maintenance.
   (b) Heat, light and power.
   (c) Benefits.
   (d) Waste and scrap.

The amount of effort required to complete a sound production plan will depend on how much production is to be farmed out. It also will depend on the nature of the product, as illustrated by the following examples.

An ice cream manufacturing plant requires equipment to mix the products and to chill the mixture, air compressors to inject air into the ice cream mix and piping to convey the ice cream mixture while it is in a fluid state. The plant also needs equipment to package the ice cream and large freezers for storage. Refrigerated trucks for delivering the product are also required. An ice cream plant is best viewed as a process requiring process control. A large plant will be capital, rather than labor intensive. A small producer is likely to use batch processing, having a somewhat higher labor cost and lower capital investment. In some ways the ice cream plant is analogous to a chemical plant.

A manufacturer of printers (such as those used with computers) requires engineering and engineering documentation to describe each part, each subassembly and the final assembly. From these documents manufacturing engineering needs to decide how each part is to be made, together with the required tooling and processes. A "make" versus "buy" decision should be made for each part. Plant layouts need to be prepared and equipment purchased and installed. Methods need to be established and documented for each operation and process. A quality plan needs to be formulated and established. A system for issuing instructions to the factory floor needs to be established. A choice will need to be made between issuing paper to the factory or installing an information system (a computer and data processing network). Materials management systems need to be established for purchasing materials (parts or assemblies) and for maintaining control over raw and work in process inventory, and for managing production runs of different models. The printer manufacturer must deal with many more parts and many more variables than the producer of ice cream.

A brief review of some program elements can shed light on a few of the decisions that must be made when preparing the production plan.

Resolving plant location issues.

The first step will be to decide where the plant will be located. The natural inclination is to locate the plant near the residences of current employees. Before reaching this conclusion it is important to examine labor and material costs and the proximity of the proposed plant site to the market. Locating a labor intensive production facility in the midst of a high labor cost area, may not be wise unless the required skills are not easily found elsewhere. Conversely, locating a plant in a low labor cost area while incurring high transportation costs also may not be wise. Some plants by their nature, should be located near their markets. Cement or service locations are examples.

The proximity of organization components to each other also should be considered. Engineering and manufacturing should be located together. Marketing and accounting can be separated from engineering and manufacturing, although there will be a penalty in the form of more difficult communications.

A logical plan to accommodate both the interests of existing employees and the long term interests of the company, might be to locate the initial plant near existing employees. The production of labor intensive components and subassemblies could be located in a remote facility, having low labor rates, later. The components and subassemblies scheduled for production at the remote facility could initially be purchased from outside vendors.

The greater the capital investment the more difficult it will be to correct a mistake if the wrong location is selected. Leasing of the plant is frequently a good tactic. Leasing should nearly always be accompanied by options to purchase the land and building and to renew the lease. Without this protection the rent may be raised to an exorbitant level when it is prohibitively expensive for the company to relocate. Also, net-net leases are usually preferable to those where the landlord pays for maintenance, leasehold improvements, taxes or other services.

Insist on flexible manufacturing.

Facilities and equipment can represent major investments. Consideration should be given to initially acquiring equipment critical to maintaining quality or protect a proprietary process. At this stage any investment in equipment should be recovered in less than two years. Some processes, such as plating, represent large environmental risks, from the spilling and disposal of chemicals and hazardous materials. In such instances it is usually better to farm out the work than to incur the investment and risk associated with the process.

An important guideline for every equipment purchasing decision, is to attempt to keep the equipment and process as flexible as possible. A single purpose piece of equipment (such as for inertia welding) can become an expensive albatross if the design needs to be changed. A flexible factory is an important objective since it is best able to support growth. Examples of how to build flexibility into a factory include: Install equipment with flexible bus-duct rather than hardwiring it in place. Use bearing mounts instead of foundations whenever possible. Use portable offices, similar to trailers, for foremen and plant management rather than building offices for them. Locate difficult to move equipment such as ovens, clean rooms and impregnation tanks as close to outside walls as possible.

The CEO should insist on the making of many layouts. Everyone, including direct labor employees, should have an opportunity to review and comment on the layout before it is completed. The best layout is seldom the creation of a single manufacturing engineer.

Build in, low operating costs.

Expenses associated with each product or service plan should be carefully scrutinized. The cost of operating and maintaining some processes can far exceed depreciation or labor costs. Heat treating or baking ovens and plating processes are examples where expenses are high.

Heat, light and power can be expensive even without ovens or special processes. The higher the bays the more expensive it will be to heat the plant. Ceiling mounted destratification fans should be used in bays over fourteen feet high.

Fluorescent lighting should be used in low bays, and high intensity discharge lighting used in high bays. The exact choice of lighting should depend on the initial cost of fixtures and lamps, the cost of power consumed and whether the quality of light (foot candles and color rendering) is important. In many locations electronic ballasts for fluorescent lighting will save enough on power costs to pay for themselves in less than two years. Compact fluorescent should be used in place of incandescent lamps, except where spotlighting or high levels of light are required. Local utilities may contribute toward the purchase of power saving equipment (such as electronic ballasts) and should be contacted for their assistance in this regard. Local utilities may charge penalties for peak demands or for high power factor. Both should be investigated and load shedding or power factor correction installed, if appropriate.

Waste can have value.

Manufacturing engineering should establish methods that reduce waste or scrap. High value materials, such as gold, silver and copper, should be collected and sold. The sale of high value scrap should be to the high bidder. Bids can be based on the London metals market, or another known and reliable basis. If the scrap has significant value, never let the scrap dealer weigh the material himself, and rotate employees who check the scrap dealer. Scrap is an often overlooked gold mine.

Manage hazardous waste, or else.

Another factor that needs to be considered is the collection and disposal of hazardous waste. This can be an expensive task fraught with legal ramifications. The CEO should determine whether the company will be using hazardous materials or generating hazardous waste. He must be certain these materials are properly handled, stored and disposed of.

Beware the hidden costs of offshore sourcing.

When deciding whether to subcontract work, especially to the far east or other low cost areas of the world, two additional factors should be included in the evaluation. The first is the inventory lock up resulting from the time required to ship product from distant countries. The second is the cash required for letters of credit. Large companies may not be required to deposit the full amount of the letter of credit in the issuing bank. An established company may only be required to deposit an amount equal to 25% of the letter of credit. A new company is frequently required to deposit the full amount; and, although the money earns interest, it cannot be used for any other purpose. In effect, the deposit is the same as tying up money in inventory.

ACTIONS TO CONSIDER TAKING.

1. Prepare the production or service plan.

The preceding brief outline of some important aspects of a production plan, highlight the complexity of the process and emphasizes the importance of thoroughness.

The nature of the product and the amount of work to be done in house, will also help to define the organization structure. Integration between engineering and manufacturing is essential. The CEO should insist on this integration in terms of organization structure and physical office location.

The production plan should evaluate how quickly the company can respond if orders are more than forecast, either by investing in additional equipment for bottleneck operations or by farming out additional work to subcontractors. This analysis may allow the CEO to select a smaller initial investment, knowing that production can be rapidly increased if demand is greater than forecast.

The production plan commits the company to a path that is frequently difficult to modify and that can have major ramifications on the company's success. Although the plan should be developed by professionals, the CEO must monitor progress and provide direction and leadership to assure that the plan is consistent with available resources and meshes with other elements of the company's strategic plan.

2. Validate the sales forecast.

Sales or order forecasts play a critical role in operating decisions. These forecasts can impact the size of the investment in plant and equipment, the amount of finished goods inventory and the number of employees.

Products with long lead times will result in order backlogs that make the task of forecasting direct labor and inventory requirements somewhat easier. Conversely this type of product frequently requires larger investments in plant and equipment, which are also long lead time items, making accurate forecasts essential.

Inaccurate forecasts can result in too much or too little investment. Too much investment penalizes profits and consumes cash for the wrong purposes. Too little investment can result in lower sales than might otherwise have been possible and may provide a competitor with an opportunity to capture a larger share of the market.

Seasonal businesses will be affected differently by inaccurate forecasts. Typically these products are built for inventory in anticipation of sales, forecast for the peak selling periods. Toys inventoried for Christmas sales are an example. Another is distribution transformers used by electric utilities to distribute electricity to residential and commercial customers.

The total market for distribution transformers depends largely on new housing and commercial construction and on high summer temperatures causing overloaded existing units to fail. The construction program at many utilities takes place during good weather, and often coincides with hot summer temperatures. The greatest usage of distribution transformers, therefore, takes place from May through September.

The inventory of distribution transformers is increased from January through April, based on the sales forecast for the year. If the sales forecast is too low, sales and market share can be lost to competitors. If the forecast is too high, too many units will be built for inventory. This results in cash being tied up in inventory and in work force disruptions when employees are laid off to decrease the level of inventory.

If the product is also susceptible to annual design or fashion trends (such as clothing, furniture, toys, and automobiles) the excess inventory must be sold at distressed prices or scrapped, possibly resulting in losses.

Service businesses frequently have extremely short lead times for their services, resulting in low backlogs of 30 to 90 days. Low sales forecasts can result in too few trained employees and excessive overtime costs. Forecasts that are too high can result in laying off trained employees in whom the company has invested heavily.

The penalty for inaccurate forecasts can be great, so it is important to use the takeoff stage to develop and validate sales forecasting techniques. Since sales forecasts are not infallible, operations should prepare contingency plans that can be used to respond to major changes in demand.

3. Establish measurements for Operations.

Measurements for quality and expenses should have been established during the start-up stage. The CEO should now work with operations to identify the key result areas for which operating measurements should be established. These measurements should allow the CEO to delegate operating decisions with the knowledge that important problems will be flagged for his attention. These measurements should be developed during the takeoff stage and be fully implemented as the company enters the growth stage.

A second level of more detailed measurements can be put in place for use by operating management to monitor the manufacturing or production process.

The CEO also can use the key result measurements to evaluate the performance of operating management. The key result measurements should be on the CEO's desk at least monthly, shortly after closing the books. The second tier of measurements should be referred to periodically or whenever a key result measurement flags a problem.

The CEO also should be certain that the second tier of measurements reflects the needs of operating management. All too often, operating management must use reports prepared by accounting for the financial organization rather than reports tailored to the needs of operations. The CEO should be certain that finance and data processing are properly oriented to the needs of operations.

Examples of both types of measurements are shown in figure 11 for manufacturing and product service businesses. (Sales by product line or by line of service should already be available.)

4. Review the design.

The takeoff stage provides an appropriate time to conduct a design review where customer and other feedback can be systematically considered. Most changes have been held in abeyance so as not to dissipate engineering resources or burden the organization with changes.

If no serious quality problems have arisen during the start-up and takeoff stages, the primary emphasis of the design review will be to identify cost and quality improvements.

Ideally this review should take place in parallel with the development of the production plan, (figure 12.) If the design review takes place after development of the production plan, changes in the design could affect equipment and layout decisions.

The design review probably will result in some basic change that should be thoroughly tested and developed to assure producibility and quality. By now document control procedures should have been implemented to maintain complete control over the design engineering, manufacturing engineering and production process.

OPERATING MEASUREMENTS		
	Manufacturing business.	Service business.
Key Result Measurements.	1. Quality. 2. Unit cost. 3. Delivery promises. 4. Finished goods inventory. 5. Work in process inventory. 6. Safety. 7. Productivity. 8. Employee turnover. 9. Investment budget.	1. Quality. 2. Unit cost. 3. Response time. 4. Parts inventory. 5. Safety. 6. Productivity. 7. Employee turnover. 8. Expense budgets. 9. Investment budget.
Other Measurements.	1. In process quality control. 2. Downtime. (Outages, shortages, etc.) 3. Variances. 4. Scrap & waste. 5. Grievances. 6. Expense budget, by line item. 7. Cost improvements.	1. Customer phone waiting time. 2. Travel time to job site. 3. Inventory obsolescence. 4. Job costs. 5. Ratio, direct to indirect labor. 6. Compensation & benefits. 7. Scrap income. 8. Overtime. 9. Sales and margin by type of work. 10. Expense budget by line item. 11. Cost improvements.

Figure 11

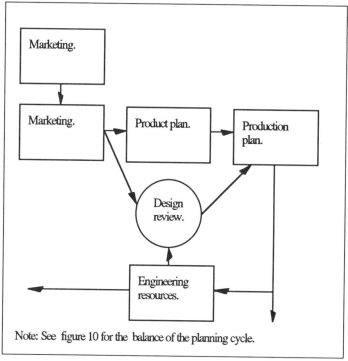

Figure 12

Figure 13 partially depicts the steps required for control. All minor changes also must be handled through the process illustrated in figure 14, though it may not be necessary to build prototype units and conduct life tests when changes are minor.

A major design change always runs the risk of problems in production and the CEO should be certain that operations has complete control over the production process before introducing the new design. Properly done the new design will result in lower costs and improved quality. Improperly done the redesigned product can result in poor quality, shipping delays, loss of customer good will, and increased manufacturing costs for rework, scrap, and poor productivity.

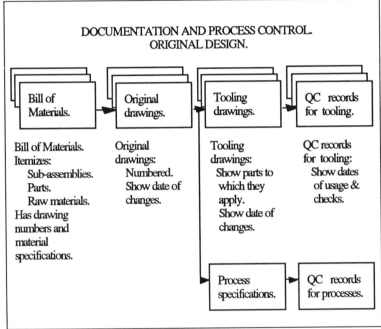

Figure 13

5. Prevent inventory buildup.

Cash remains a critical asset during the takeoff stage and inventory levels should be closely managed. Equally important is the impact that the redesigned product will have on inventories. When making major changes to the design, it is important to manage the transition from old to new models so as not to have obsolete inventory (either finished goods or work in process) on hand when the introduction is complete.

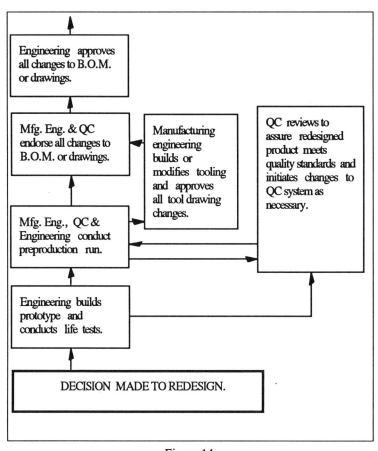

Figure 14

Section Five

People

Three key organization principles.

As the company evolves through the takeoff stage, the CEO will need to give attention to organization structure. The natural tendency of an entrepreneur turned CEO is to decry organization charts as a bureaucratic encumbrance.

With growth, organization structure is inevitable; and it's better for the CEO to address the issue early and establish a structure that is best for the company.

There are three organization principles that can be endorsed by the CEO, regardless of the company's business.

1. Have as broad a span of control as possible for every manager or supervisor, at every level in the organization.

2. Have as few organization levels as possible. (The first principle leads naturally to the second.)

3. Adopt a "one over one" policy for approvals involving people (for actions such as salary, hiring, and managerial awards), and where such actions are not established by policy (such as for vacations, benefits, etc.).

A span of control of ten is not unreasonable, and can sometimes be even broader. First line supervisors and foremen can be expected to have twenty or more employees reporting to them. The number of employees reporting to first line management can vary widely depending on the complexity or technical content of the work. Situations requiring considerable technical input from the supervisor could have fewer people reporting to the supervisor while a simple production line operation could have forty employees reporting to the foreman. For other than first line management, the CEO should think in terms of ten direct reports for each manager.

There are several reasons why ten is an appropriate span of control. A wide span of control throughout the organization automatically results in fewer organization layers. This is an important consideration in that it reduces the communications problem for the CEO.

The more organization layers through which the message must be transmitted, the greater the probability of the message being distorted before it reaches the lower levels of the organization; which is where most of the day to day action takes place. The CEO wants his message concerning the company's strategic direction and of the actions required to achieve success, to be received loud and clear by everyone.

A wide span of control also results in fewer managers (which improves communications) and lower overhead costs. Assume that a manager earns $50,000. Add approximately 30% for benefits. Also add the salary and benefits for a secretary amounting to approximately $25,000. Then add heat, light, phones and travel and living expenses, and the annual savings from preventing the addition of one manager can easily be $100,000.

A third benefit of a broad span of control is that it forces managers to delegate, which gives everyone in the organization more freedom and creates more interesting jobs.

A fourth advantage to a broad span of control is that it can help assure the development of people and fairness in administering people oriented issues. To accomplish this, the CEO must establish the practice of having every manager get to know those who report directly to them and also those in the next lower organization layer. This means that each manager, including the CEO, must become familiar with the performance, capabilities, strengths, weaknesses, and aspirations of approximately 100 people.

When it comes time to fill a vacancy, the manager can select from people he knows well or from people recommended by other managers, who also know their people equally well.

By insisting on a broad span of control and on each manager knowing the people in the two organization layers below them, there will be little need to establish a manpower organization to look after those who should or should not be promoted.

The complexity of relationships between managers also should be considered when establishing the span of control. A supervisor who must spend considerable time interfacing with manufacturing engineering, concerning methods and standards, may not be able to supervise as many employees as usual. It's still better to assume that cross relationships have a minimum impact until proven otherwise.

SPAN OF CONTROL Unadjusted	
NUMBER OF EMPLOYEES AT EACH LEVEL.	AVERAGE SPAN
1	10
10	10
100	10
1000	

Figure 15

Figure 15 shows an organization with a uniform span of control of ten. Figure 16 shows an organization that attempts to have a broad span of control but, as is often true, falls slightly short of the goal. A successful manufacturing or product service company should realize sales of at least $100,000 per employee.

SPAN OF CONTROL Adjusted	
NUMBER OF EMPLOYEES AT EACH LEVEL.	AVERAGE SPAN.
1	5
5	8
40	15
600	
Note: Typical organization will probably not be symmetrical. More organization layers may be required in manufacturing. Geographic considerations can also result in narrower spans.	

Figure 16

It is entirely possible for a company with sales of between $5 and $50 million to have a maximum of three organization layers below the CEO; and for a company with sales of $100 to $600 million to have no more than four organization layers below the CEO.

During the takeoff stage the CEO should visualize how his organization structure might look when sales reach $100 million and also at one or two intermediate levels. This will provide a guide for additional positions that might be added as the company grows beyond the takeoff stage.

The Marketing VP, for example, can directly manage the sales force of a $5 to $10 million company. At some point it will be necessary to add one or more sales managers. Similarly the manager of manufacturing may eventually need a manager of materials. After considering how the organization is likely to evolve, the CEO can establish an initial organization structure that takes some of these evolutionary changes into consideration. Realizing that a position must be established during the following year, the CEO may decide to fill the position now with a very narrow span of control and add, what might otherwise appear to be, an extra layer of management. He would then allow the organization to fill around the original structure until a broad span of control is achieved.

This will raise an important issue for the CEO, since some people who report directly to him now, may not do so in the future. The company may add a sales manager during the start-up or takeoff stage who may not become the Marketing VP when that position is filled. Showing an open position for the VP of Marketing prevents misunderstandings and possible embarrassment for the sales manager. An alternative is for the sales manager to be appointed acting Marketing VP so that he has sufficient influence with outside parties. It should remain clear to everyone though, that the Marketing VP position is not yet filled.

It is also important that persons in an acting capacity know exactly where they stand. They should be told whether they will be candidates for the position. This is especially true for those who are newly hired into the organization, otherwise seeds of discontent will have been sewn. Handling these issues is a difficult task involving personal interfaces between the manager and the person involved. Some managers are uncomfortable in this role and may omit important parts of the communication. They may not, for example, tell the person hired as sales manager that he will not be considered for Marketing VP. (The person also should be told why he won't be considered.)

The CEO can assure himself that an open discussion has taken place by asking the newly hired manager questions such as: "I suppose Frank explained to you how we intend to organize his department over the next few months?" Once everyone knows that the CEO will probably follow up with a question such as this, they will be more likely to handle difficult communications (including salary and performance appraisals) more openly.

Managing with a broad span of control is facilitated by having a one over one approval policy. Performance appraisals, salary adjustments, promotions, managerial awards etc. should all require one over one approval. With this in place the manager must review his recommendations with his immediate superior before advising the employee. This helps to assure fairness, which is an important issue for the CEO.

ACTIONS TO CONSIDER TAKING.

1. Establish a compensation and salary plan.

As previously mentioned such a plan is essential to assure fairness as the organization grows. The compensation plan probably will require the approval of the board of directors, especially if stock options are involved.

The compensation and salary plan does not have to be complicated but should provide:

1. Salary ranges that recognize different levels of performance, from satisfactory to outstanding.

2. Several salary levels within each organization level.

3. An approach for recognizing exceptional performance within the year with bonuses or stock options.

Figure 17 depicts a simple approach to meeting these criteria, though there are professional groups who can develop other structures that may be more appropriate for the company. The numbers in the sample structure are not important per se, though the relationships are. Besides the salary structure illustrated by figure 17, an hourly wage structure can be

developed where the higher hourly rates overlap the lower
levels of the exempt salary structure.

EXEMPT SALARY STRUCTURE					
Position Step.	Base Salary 100%	Performance range as % of base salary in dollars.			
		110%	120%	130%	140%
15	$70,128	77,140	84,153	91,166	98,179
14	$65,540	72,094	78,648	85,202	91,756
13	$61,252	67,377	73,503	79,628	85,753
12	$57,245	62,970	68,694	74,419	80,143
11	$53,500	58,850	64,200	69,550	74,900
10	$50,000	55,000	60,000	65,000	70,000
9	$45,160	49,617	54,128	58,638	63,149
8	$38,226	42,048	45,871	49,693	53,516
7	$32,395	35,634	38,874	42,113	45,353
6	$27,453	30,198	32,944	35,689	38,434
5	$23,265	25,592	27,918	30,245	32,571
4	$19,716	21,688	23,660	25,631	27,603
3	$16,709	18,380	20,051	21,721	23,392
2	$14,160	15,576	16,992	18,408	19,824
1	$12,000	13,200	14,400	15,600	16,800

Figure 17

The sample exempt salary structure begins with the
lowest position (step 1 in this example) and progresses to the
highest for the CEO (step 15). Employees whose jobs are rated
a particular step, can be paid any salary within the step, which
in the example ranges from 100% to 140% of the base salary.
Presumably employees would be promoted before reaching the
highest salary within each step.

Positions step 9 and below are on a straight salary, while
those above step 9 receive a significant part of their
compensation as stock options. Each step from 10 to 15 would
be eligible for increasingly larger amounts of stock options. For

example positions at step 10 could be eligible to receive up to 5000 shares of stock while positions at step 14 could be eligible for up to 30,000 shares of stock. The precise amount awarded each year would be approved by the board of directors and be based on performance. The spread between the base salaries of steps 10 through 15, is roughly half the spread between base salaries below step 10. This is to recognize that senior management compensation is tied to overall company performance with stock options providing an incentive to improve company performance.

The exempt salary plan permits salaries to be based on performance, with all steps in the structure having a salary range of 40% from the base salary to the highest salary within a step. Consistently satisfactory performance would be rewarded by a salary between 100 and 110% of the base. Consistently outstanding performance would be rewarded by a salary of between 130 and 140% of the base.

The exempt salary structure allows jobs with varying degrees of importance or complexity, and differing ranges of salary, to report to the same manager. The Marketing VP could be a position step 14, while the other positions reporting to him could have job positions with the steps shown below. Eastern sales manager, step 12: Western sales manager, step 10: Manager of product planning, step 13: Supervisor of order service, step 7.

The salary structure also can accommodate changes in the importance of a position as the company grows. In the previous example the Western sales manager's position could be increased to step 12. The reevaluation would be based on increases in the number of salesmen reporting to him and the size of the accounts for which he is responsible. Arriving at the proper step rating for each position may require assistance from an outside firm skilled in establishing salary structures. Jobs within a function and between functions require some basis for determining their relative worth. The salary range established for each position also should be competitive with comparable jobs in the industry.

The plan also would permit managerial awards or bonuses to employees who are not eligible for stock options, so that management can reward unusually outstanding performance.

2. Encourage open communications.

As the company progresses through the takeoff stage the number of new employees who must be assimilated by the organization will increase. The CEO will want to exert his influence and style on new employees. He will want to instill in them the same enthusiasm for the business he has, and maintain their focus on the company's objectives. When there were only a dozen or so employees, as was true during the start-up stage, communications could be informal and impromptu. By the end of the takeoff stage the company could have a hundred employees. With one hundred employees it is more difficult to arrange gatherings that afford opportunities for open communications that help build moral and a team with a corporate personality. The problem gets considerably more vexing as the number of employees increases further. The CEO must find ways to continue meeting with employees monthly, until it becomes physically impractical.

During the takeoff stage monthly meetings can be arranged that afford opportunities for team building. These could include picnics, team sports, or field trips to suppliers or places having an important bearing on the company. It is not too difficult to find space for a meeting where the CEO can address the entire group and respond to questions. The CEO also can use these occasions to arrange for special recognition of employees who have made important contributions to the company.

Making certain that these meetings take place and that he plays an important and visible role at each meeting is important to the CEO. Besides affording him an opportunity to discuss his views and vision for the company, it also allows him to learn first hand the concerns and views of the employees. The CEO can listen carefully to what employees are saying in an informal atmosphere. In this atmosphere he will learn things that he can learn in no other way. Some of what he learns must be handled with discretion so as not to violate the trust people may place in him. More often than not the CEO and other managers will learn much and be given many good ideas.

3. Avoid setting salaries too high.

The company must guard against establishing position steps and salaries that are not commensurate with the size and importance of jobs as they currently exist.

Besides using outside assistance to establish the salary structure, every new position or change in a position's evaluation, should require the approval of the CEO. The CEO will always want to maintain some involvement in this process though he will need to delegate more authority in the setting of salary levels as the company grows.

Pricing is not a science. Pricing is an art that has a direct bearing on the growth and profitability of a company.

Without control over inventory the CEO cannot manage cash flow, and if he cannot manage cash flow he risks everything.

THE GROWTH STAGE.

Section One

Cash

Managing cash.

The growth stage will place major demands on cash; and, rather than easing the pressure on the CEO for husbanding cash, will merely shift the emphasis to cash management.

The major uses of cash during the growth stage will be for inventories, receivables and investment in equipment. Product service businesses are likely also to require considerable cash for training.

The CEO, with his Chief Financial Officer, will need to make detailed cash flow projections based on forecast sales and operating expenses. Figure 18 depicts a process for developing cash flow projections. It will be based on projections for sales, cost of sales, and expenses, and assumptions for items such as interest rates and days of receivables outstanding.

Personal computers have made the preparation of detailed spreadsheets very easy. The program for producing spreadsheets should be fully integrated. Changes to any input, such as the number of salesmen or a salesman's salary, should automatically change the operating statement, balance sheet, and cash flow statement. Statements can be run to show monthly or quarterly projections.

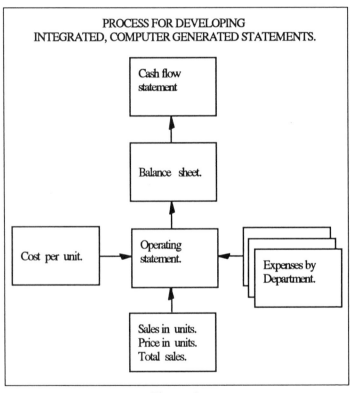

Figure 18

The CEO should be personally involved in the preparation of these statements, making the final decision with respect to each assumption. He should understand the interaction between expenses, cost of sales, inventories etc., in order to make informed decisions on how to allocate resources (specifically cash). The CEO can gain these insights by working with the program himself; making changes in the various assumptions.

While programs of this type are very helpful, the CEO should be careful to recognize that the spreadsheets do not reflect the gospel truth; and cannot predict the future. Sales may deviate considerably from the projections. Inventories may bulge. Customers may not pay their bills on time. Or a dozen other factors can change the outcome generated by the program. A strategic reserve or back up position should always be a part of the CEO's decision making process.

Cash flow projections generated by the program will allow the CEO and CFO to estimate the company's borrowing requirements, and whether additional equity funds will be needed. These same projections can be used with the company's banker to establish the necessary line of credit. In addition the cash flow projection may show that the production plan must be adjusted to reduce the investment in plant and equipment - or conversely, show that money is available to pursue key cost improvement opportunities.

The danger of optimizing the sub-optimum.

Another important consideration during the growth stage is the ever increasing number of employees. As the organization grows it may become more functionally oriented, where the employees have a narrower view of the business. Employees who were with the business during the start-up and takeoff stages will have a common understanding of the company's objectives coupled with an insight into all the various functions. Many original employees will have worn multiple hats, working in several functions, such as marketing, production, engineering, etc.

New employees are not likely to have the same views and will be more oriented to the function in which they work, perceiving success in terms of the success of the function rather than the business. Their personal success and advancement will depend on how well they do their jobs - which, inescapably, is translated into how well their department does. This can result in people making decisions that optimize the sub-optimum.

The experience of a major multiproduct, multinational company with subsidiaries in a dozen important countries around the world, illustrates this point. The issue was whether each subsidiary should develop and implement a strategy that would maximize its potential in each individual country's small market (as compared to the world market for each product), or whether worldwide strategies should be developed for each product line to maximize the worldwide potential of the parent company.

The answer in this example (as is often true) was not as straight forward as it might first seem. Other important factors had to be considered, not the least of which were laws on local content and currency control.

Any decentralized organization can experience the problem of having a component optimize its own results to the detriment of the company's total results. This becomes an organizational issue that the CEO must consider as he formulates the organization structure that will carry the company through the growth stage.

Similarly, functions tend to make decisions from the perspective of their function. Purchasing or production control could use text book approaches when deciding how many of a certain part to purchase or build.

A typical formula $EOQ = (2CN/PI + 2FA)^{1/2}$ (see appendix), purports to show the quantity to be ordered to arrive at the lowest unit cost. It also results, however, in an inventory buildup that uses cash. The purchasing or production department will be commended on the cost reduction that results from such an approach. But cash that could have been used elsewhere, will be tied up in inventory.

Similarly, requests for equipment and people may be based on what is perceived to be important for the function, and these priorities may not be consistent with those of the CEO. The growth stage requires, therefore, that systems and budgets be in place to assure control and to allow the CEO to establish priorities.

The CEO must always have sufficient cash to meet his payroll and pay suppliers in a reasonable period; or the company goes bankrupt. Simplistic as this sounds, it is amazing how frequently companies have problems in meeting these commitments. Worlds of Wonder, Storage Technology, Televideo and Datapoint are highly publicized examples of growth companies who, for one reason or another, had cash flow problems.

As the company continues to be successful it may amass cash reserves and pay off some of its debt. Some businesses, however, will continue to use cash as long as they grow. Rental and leasing businesses are examples where rapid growth requires investment in new equipment (to be rented or leased to others) exceeding the combined cash flow generated by profits and depreciation.

When the company's balance sheet improves, and cash reserves are generated, the CEO should decide how best to use cash as a strategic resource.

ACTIONS TO CONSIDER TAKING.

1. Keep budgets simple.

Expense budgets should initially have been established during the takeoff stage when there were few employees and the budgets could be simple and straight forward. With an ever increasing number of employees during the growth stage, the budget process itself deserves attention.

Many theories have been touted for the budgeting process; such as, top down, bottom up, fixed, variable, stepped, program, and zero base budgeting (see figure 19). Whatever the process, it should meet certain criteria. It should:

(a) Reflect the CEO's priorities (which should reflect the company's strategy).

(b) Recognize the limited availability of resources.

(c) Reflect the requirements of each function so that they may be effective in doing their job.

(d) Recognize that each function must achieve productivity improvements and cost reductions from one year to the next.

(e) Be kept as simple as possible.

Once the budget has been established it must be accounted for, reported on, measured and used. Variances must be identified and acted upon. For greatest usefulness in monitoring operations the reports showing actual expenses versus budgeted expenses should be issued monthly, within a few days of the preceding months closing. All this requires administrative expense, and a bureaucracy. The simpler the budget system the easier it is to administer.

For example, program budgets are sometimes used to allocate resources to a program (new product, new process, new plant, etc.), and to keep program costs separated from regular operating expenses. It is often a good approach for focusing resources and maintaining priorities. On the other hand program budgets can be used as a dumping ground for what might otherwise be considered routine operating expenses. To keep the various functions from overcharging the program, administrative routines must be put in place to monitor and

TYPES OF EXPENSE BUDGETS

FIXED:

Sales are forecast for the year and allocated by month.
Expense budgets are established based on forecast sales.
Simplest type of budget to administer.

VARIABLE:

High and low sales forecasts are made for the year.
Expense budgets are established for the range of sales.
Expense budget varies with actual sales.
Very difficult to administer.

STEP:

High and low sales forecasts are made for the year and then
broken into steps within the high and low forecasts.
Expenses are budgeted for each step in the sales forecast.
Both the sales and expense budgets are allocated by month.
The expense budget used for the month is the step that matches
the actual sales for the month.
This type of budget accomplishes much of what the variable
budget does, but is easier to administer.

TOP DOWN AND BOTTOM UP BUDGETING PROCESS:

Top down refers to budgets established by the CEO.
Bottom up refers to budgets that are established within a
function based on the sales forecast. A combination of top down
and bottom up budgeting can provide a budget that meets the
CEO's objectives as well as the needs of the functions.
Budget itself can be fixed, variable, or step.

ZERO BASE BUDGET:

Process requires that each function build its budget from a
zero base. The function assumes that it starts the year
without funding and then justifies each expense.
Budget itself can be fixed, variable, or step.

PROGRAM:

A separate budget is established for each program in addition
to each functions' budget. This allows resources to be allocated to
high priority projects.

Figure 19

approve the expenses charged to the program. This in turn leads to disputes and management time to resolve them.

In addition to selecting and establishing the budgeting process that will best suit his company, the CEO also must decide how actively he will participate in the budget setting process. Being too involved stifles initiative and leaves the organization believing that the budget is the CEO's responsibility and not theirs. If people in the organization haven't "bought off" on the budget, they will be less committed to its realization.

Lack of involvement by the CEO can, however, result in misapplied resources or waste. One of the CEO's responsibilities is to exercise leadership in establishing doable, but hard to reach goals. Without such a challenge, budgets will become fat.

Watch those receivables and inventories.

The CEO can never lose sight of the importance of personally monitoring receivables and inventories, making certain that the Marketing, Manufacturing and Engineering Vice Presidents do likewise. Receivables should be classified by age and amount (as described earlier). Inventories (total and by model) should be compared against budget and monitored on the basis of number of days sales.

Marketing should be imbued with the philosophy that the sale is not complete until the cash is in the till. Many overdue receivables are the result of misunderstandings or dissatisfaction, and the salesman is in the best position to get to the bottom of the problem and have the situation corrected. If the customer cannot be satisfied the invoice will have to be adjusted and a write down taken. Any such write down should be approved by the Marketing VP, with a record kept of all such adjustments, classified by salesman and customer, for periodic review by the CEO.

3. Avoid frills.

As the company grows and prospers the pressures on the CEO to loosen control over non essential expenditures can become overwhelming. Larger and plushier offices, country club memberships, company cars, magazine subscriptions, personal secretaries and a host of other worthwhile suggestions will be floated by the CEO. The CEO must resist these overtures while not assuming the role of Scrooge. Similarly the temptation to add staff will be equally great, and should be equally resisted.

To the extent possible, the CEO should require that each proposal be judged on a cost benefit basis. He should make it clear he will look with considerable displeasure on frivolous proposals. Purchase of company cars, for example, can be evaluated by comparing the amount of reimbursement for company mileage to the annual ownership costs if the car was to be purchased by the company. Such an evaluation quickly eliminates most of management and usually limits company cars to salesmen and service technicians or service engineers.

Whatever the CEO approves will become institutionalized in the company's cost structure and be very difficult to eliminate in the future.

Section Two

Strategy

The strategic planning process.

It has already been shown that the development of a strategic plan with its component parts, is a reiterative process. The marketing plan, the product plan, and the production plan are all mutually interdependent: and are collectively dependent on the availability of resources.

The question which comes first, product planning, market planning or production planning, is irrelevant. What is important to the CEO is that the process is defined and that all functions participate. The process itself can be triggered each year by the CEO establishing initial guidelines with respect to resource allocations and sales volume, and restating his near and long term vision for the business.

The near term vision is basically how to make the most from the initial product or service. The long term vision defines how the company can grow through the addition of new products, new markets or new services.

In the early years of the growth stage the emphasis will be on the near term strategy, with a conceptual overview of the longer term strategy. As market penetration is achieved with the initial product or service, the longer term strategy must come into sharper focus. Eventually the initial product or market will mature and growth will flatten. New products or services must be added if the company is to continue to grow. It can be viewed as a series of S curves added one on top of the other, which cumulatively represent the growth of the company.

The strategic plan of a service company could have two dimensions besides near and long term strategies: (1) Geographic growth by expanding into new service territories,

(2) Product line growth by adding new types of products to those initially being serviced.

The service company with a limited type of product, for example AT&T PBX phone switches, may have started by serving only three territories, Denver Colorado, Lincoln Nebraska, and Wichita Kansas. This hypothetical company can expand into new territories, such as Casper Wyoming and Colorado Springs Colorado; and can add new products to its service line, such as printers and computers. (Or it could add chicken sandwiches to its initial offer of hamburgers if the service business was a fast food restaurant.)

The strategic plan should define how both expansions should take place, given the available resources. One plan could call for the establishment of cornerstone service centers in major cities. These locations would provide the necessary technical, administrative and inventory support for satellite operations ringing the cornerstone locations. Another strategy could call for a linked diversification between products that are to be serviced, where the technologies are related, to minimize training and inventory costs. Another strategy could call for becoming the product service arm for several manufacturers, based on the density of the products in each service territory.

Any or all of these strategies could be adopted, but it is unlikely the company will have the resources to adopt all of them. In addition there could easily be environmental factors that make one approach riskier than another.

Attempting to expand geographically into Vancouver Canada, might cause the company (in the hypothetical example) to run afoul of Canadian agencies regulating the telephone industry. This environmental issue should be investigated before adopting a strategy of international expansion.

Every business will have its own unique issues that must be considered when developing its strategy. Some products, for example, may not be suitable for shipping long distances. Ice cream, various wines, and cement are examples where cost or quality may be a problem when the product is shipped a long distance. The availability of raw materials or power may dictate the location of manufacturing plants: Steel and aluminum are examples. Governments may regulate the industry. Postal and telephone service, foods and drugs are examples of regulated industries in most countries of the world.

Development of a strategy that carries the company beyond its initial product or service is essential if the CEO wants to maintain growth. Other considerations besides developing a strategic plan include:

ACTIONS TO CONSIDER TAKING

1. Consider vertical integration to increase profits.

A study by a Fortune 100 company determined that there was a correlation between high contributed value and high profitability for its many product businesses. This should not be unexpected since supplier profits and overhead are eliminated when work is done in house, providing the volume is great enough to warrant the necessary investment.

If cost and quality can be improved, and if resources become available, the CEO should consider increasing the amount of contributed value, once the company is safely in the growth stage.

2. Segment your market.

The CEO should be certain that the marketing plan has segmented the market when arriving at its market and product plans. Besides basic models meeting the functional requirements of the product, additional models could be added having premium features that command higher prices and margins. Choice of distribution channel may reflect segmenting customers by size or type of industry.

3. Define aftermarket opportunities.

These opportunities can include providing replacement parts, the sale of ancillary devices and supplies, product repair, maintenance contracts, management contracts and more. Examples include: printer ribbons (supplies), computer mouse (ancillary device), three year appliance maintenance contract, and a contract to staff and manage a cogeneration power plant.

4. Reestablish R & D priorities.

Research and development efforts can be closely related to the existing product line or can be for development of unrelated products. The CEO of a young company in the growth stage of its initial product line, should be certain that R&D activities relate directly to the company's strategy.

Very large companies can afford to do basic research having little bearing on current products, in anticipation of breakthroughs leading to new products, or to major, but unpredictable, improvements to existing products. Even large companies will tend to limit basic research to those disciplines having a direct bearing on their current businesses.

The CEO may be encouraged to allocate a certain percentage of revenues or profits to R&D, but should resist this approach. Instead he should determine what research is needed to achieve his strategy and fund it appropriately (assuming the availability of cash), whether the amount is 2% or 15% of sales.

5. Establish international priorities.

In most cases the domestic market should be developed first, and substantial market penetration achieved here before approaching foreign markets. Some reasons for this are:

(a) The domestic U.S. market is usually the largest market in the world and provides the best opportunities for identifying niches and establishing customer credibility.

(b) Cultural and other local conditions (laws, regulations etc.) are different in foreign countries, and may be difficult to understand or act upon correctly.

(c) Distances and time zone differences make communications very difficult, though much easier with the arrival of FAX machines.

(d) The cost of moving Americans to foreign locations is exorbitantly expensive, meaning less reliance on US trained employees and much greater reliance on foreign nationals. The cost of training foreign nationals is also very high if the training needs to take place in the US.

(e) The distribution system may be different, may require local partners (either due to law or local practice). There also may be a history of trade practices that are illegal in the US or contrary to US standards.

(f) The cost associated with handling warranty claims and providing service can be very high.

(g) Many countries have currency controls making it difficult to translate local currency into dollars (or other hard currencies).

The strategic plan should, in most cases, definitely envision conducting business internationally. The CEO must assure that the strategic plan establishes proper priorities for approaching the international market, and incorporates meaningful solutions to the problems itemized above.

After establishing international priorities in terms of markets, a determination should be made whether foreign subsidiaries should be established; either to penetrate the market or for manufacturing purposes.

Offshore subsidiaries also can be a source of capital to the parent company if it wishes to sell stock in its subsidiaries, on the local stock market.

6. Study your competitors and customers.

The strategic planning process should include an analysis of competitors, competitive products and competing technologies.

The CEO should also be certain that customer needs have been thoroughly evaluated during the preparation of the marketing and product plans. As previously mentioned, the CEO must take time to meet with customers to assess for himself how good a job his company is doing in serving his customers.

7. Avoid a mismatch between strategy and resources.

This is probably the single most important consideration for the CEO once he has satisfied himself that the strategic plan is meaningful and without platitudes.

A plan that deals in generalities is not going to be meaningful. "Achieve the best product on the market" or "reach a leadership position", are useless objectives.

"Produce a product that meets specific performance criteria that are superior to competitors and have the highest standard for quality as measured by an independent testing laboratory" or "achieve a market share of 60%", are objectives that can be measured and evaluated.

The CEO will need to include an objective evaluation of the availability of critical resources. These can include cash, engineers, service technicians, salesmen, or programmers. Where people are the resource in question, the cost and time required for training must be included in the evaluation. The plan may call for opening ten new cornerstone service locations in the coming year, but if trained management or technicians aren't available the new locations cannot be opened successfully. To persist in carrying out a plan without the needed resources can lead to serious complications. It is up to the CEO to satisfy himself that the resources are available to match the plan.

Section Three

Marketing

During the takeoff stage, the CEO's marketing focus was on securing initial sales for a quality product or service, and on developing a strong marketing team. In the growth stage the CEO will shift his involvement from sales per se, to product planning and strategic planning.

A Vice President of Marketing will need to be added if the CEO has been filling this role until now. The day to day supervision of the sales force and distribution channel, with the development of sales programs and new accounts, will require full time attention. During the growth stage sales will grow between 25% and 50% each year, and sometimes more. With an existing sales base of $5 to $10 million this translates into annual sales increases of $2 to $5 million, or more. A 25% growth rate will result in the company doubling in size every three years (plus a few months), while a 50% growth rate has the company doubling in size every other year. Clearly the implications for Marketing (and also Manufacturing) are enormous, not the least of which is the need for a strong management team and a very competent Marketing VP.

The CEO should, if possible, continue to retain final approval over consignment of inventory or in any changes to terms and conditions of sale.

Eleven important reports for the CEO.

The CEO will need to rely on management techniques and tools to reach his objectives. This means delegating day to day activities to Marketing, and having systems in place that allow the CEO to monitor Marketing's progress toward reaching its goals. The CEO should still play an active role in product planning (which is an integral part of strategic planning). He must also allow time to meet with customers so as not to become disengaged from the most important activity of all - serving the customer.

The CEO should have the following eleven reports on his desk at the month's end, in addition to the operating statement and balance sheet:

1. Total sales for the current month, compared with budget and the same period last year.

2. Total sales year to date, compared with budget and the same period last year.

3. Inventory for the current month compared with budget, (possibly broken down by model).

4. Sales by salesman and territory.

5. Sales by customer, grouped to reflect the sales plan to identify deviations from plan. Also a listing of the ten largest customers (perhaps in each territory or for each salesman) for the current year to date and for the same period last year.

6. Current month receivables, grouped by age. For example under 30 days, 30 to 90 days, 90 to 180 days, and over 180 days. It should also show the ten largest receivables with the name of the salesman responsible for resolving the receivable if it is overdue. (More than ten if there is a problem with total receivables.)

7. Promises kept (or similar reports for project or service type businesses).

8. A measure of pricing to indicate actual price levels. This can be percent below the book price or other meaningful measure of price. If possible the report

should be issued to show results by salesman and by customer.

9. Complaints by customer. This should include all warranty costs and all concessions. If possible, it also should include complaints that do not result in financial expenditures.

10. Marketing expenses compared with budget, for the current month and year to date.

11. Periodically (perhaps quarterly) an estimate should be made of market share.

Some of these items can be integrated into the operating statement, others will require separate reports. Industry associations may gather sales data on companies within the industry, making it somewhat easy to obtain reasonably accurate market share information; albeit sometimes out of date. If industry data is not available it will be necessary to determine sales of each competitor by analyzing their quarterly and annual reports. The information available in this manner is usually incomplete. It may be necessary to also develop statistical means for estimating market size as a cross check on the empirically derived market share.

As previously mentioned systems also should be in place to allow the CEO to participate in the pricing of large, or strategic orders.

ACTIONS TO CONSIDER TAKING.

1. Establish the marketing plan.

This plan defines how marketing is going to approach the market, and is an integral part of the corporate strategic plan.

As discussed during the start up stage, a distribution and sales plan should have been adopted during the start up stage and used (with appropriate modifications) during the takeoff stage. By now it will be clear whether the distribution channel originally established will meet the needs of the company as it plans to double in size every two to three years.

More likely than not it will be necessary to modify the distribution channel, which is why it is so important to be certain that exclusivity is not included in the original distributor and representative agreements.

A not unusual modification to the original plan is to approach major customers directly rather than relying on a distributor or representative. This may even have been the preferred sales approach from the very beginning, but lacking the financial resources to hire salesmen it was necessary to use a distributor or representative.

The marketing plan will, therefore, segment the market by size and by product variations. Refer to figure 20 for a simplified example. A service business could elect to serve customers directly in geographic territories having high sales potential, while franchising others to serve the less concentrated markets.

The marketing plan also will describe how the company will capture a share of mind. This is especially important to service businesses where the customer reacts to a momentary event, such as the failure of a piece of equipment, or the need for temporary secretarial service. The intent is for the customer to think immediately of the company by name, and to call the company without researching other possibilities. This is achieved by having performed well on a previous order, or being recommended by others based on their favorable experience or through effective advertising.

The marketing plan should define the use of indirect selling methods (such as advertising, direct mail, telemarketing, etc.) and the results to be achieved from their use.

MARKET SEGMENTATION BY CUSTOMER FOR SALES PLANNING.			
Customer locations.	Major potential customers.		All other potential customers. (b)
	Who accept current design.	Who require design changes. (a)	
Near existing sales offices.	Sell direct. (c)	Sell direct. (c)	Sell direct or through distributors or representatives. (c) (d)
Near probable location of new sales offices.	Sell direct or through distributors or representatives. (d)	Sell direct or through distributors or representatives. (d)	Sell direct or through distributors or representatives. (d)
Remote from existing or planned sales offices.	Use distributors or manufacturer representatives. (d)	Use distributors or manufacturer representatives. (d)	Use distributors or manufacturer representatives. (d)

Notes:
(a) Identify changes proposed by customers to establish priorities.
(b) Sell directly if using a distributor or manufacturers' representative makes it difficult to manage sales territory.
(c) Care should be taken in segmenting market when customers have multiple buying or influence points. At issue is who should call on each location and how distributors or manufacturer representatives receive credit when more than one sales force is involved.
(d) Distributor and manufacturer representative agreements must permit cancellation. Agreements should not be exclusive.

Figure 20

2. Planning the product line.

The product plan establishes how the product line will be expanded to include different features or fit additional applications. An electronic ballast can illustrate this point. A company might introduce an initial product line of electronic ballasts consisting of two models: A unit rated 120 volts for use with two four foot fluorescent lamps; and a second unit rated 277 volts, also for use with two four foot lamps. Figure 21 shows the array of models required to meet most standard installations. Twenty times this many models will be required to meet all the possible installation requirements for fluorescent lamps. If the electronic ballast is revolutionary and can dim fluorescent lamps, then both non-dimming and dimming designs must be developed for each model.

TYPICAL FLUORESCENT LAMP BALLAST RATINGS.			
Rated for number and length of lamp.	Watts	Volts	Start
2, 4 foot.	40	120	Rapid.
2, 4 foot.	40	277	Rapid.
1, 4 foot.	40	120	Rapid.
1, 4 foot.	40	277	Rapid.
2, 8 foot.	60/75	120	Instant.
2, 8 foot.	60/75	277	Instant.
1, 8 foot.	60/75	120	Instant.
1, 8 foot.	60/75	277	Instant.
2, 2 foot.	20	120	Rapid.
2, 2 foot.	20	277	Rapid.
4, 4 foot.	20	120	Rapid.
4, 4 foot.	20	277	Rapid.

Figure 21

The role of product planning in this situation is to establish priorities for the development of these models. For electronic ballasts, the needs are almost predetermined by the standard fixture and lamp sizes, with figure 21 representing the more common units. If customer needs have not been predetermined, product planning will have to identify each of the required features.

Because of its importance to the company, the CEO must decide how the product planning process will be accomplished. Product planning affects customer acceptance and sales, use of engineering and manufacturing resources, investment in equipment, expenses for testing and tooling, and ultimately product quality and customer satisfaction. All functions should be a party to the process due to the need for integrating their activities. Figure 22 depicts the product planning cycle that begins with customer needs, has marketing establish priorities, requires manufacturing, engineering, quality control and accounting to provide cost and scheduling information, has all functions concurring with the plan (or identifying their concerns with specific aspects of the plan) and ends with the CEO approving the plan.

The product plan and marketing plan become a part of the corporate strategic plan; the development of which may result in modifications to the product plan.

In spite of the need for the involvement of every function, Marketing (which is closest to the customer) should have the lead in determining priorities. In the 1960's the major manufacturers of distribution transformers had established the basic models offered to electric utilities. A new competitor, RTE corporation, introduced models having multiple switches (permitting the same unit to be used with two different high voltage inputs) and pad mounted transformers suited to underground distribution systems.

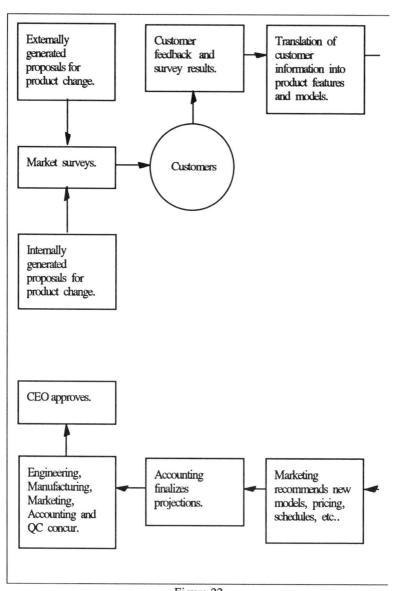

Figure 22

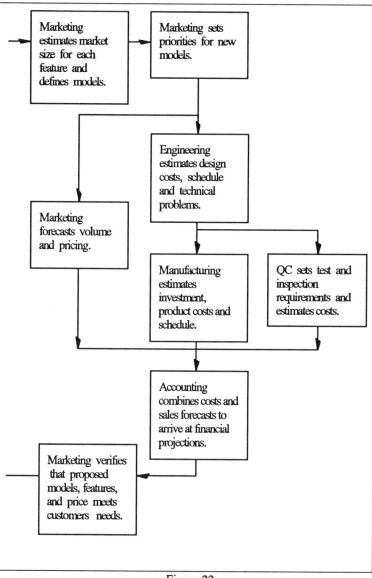

Figure 22

Product planning at a major manufacturer recommended the introduction of competing models, but engineering overruled the recommendation believing that the new models weren't necessary and were merely a fad. Eventually both types of units became industry standards and, because of its responsiveness to customer requests, RTE grew into a major supplier of distribution transformers.

Engineering or other functions who have limited views and who are frequently concerned with their functional problems, should not be allowed to overrule Marketing. In addition the CEO needs to be close enough to the market and to product planning to understand the validity of Marketings' recommendations.

In addition to Marketing having lead responsibility, the product planning process should be centralized. One of the two manufacturers of distribution transformers referred to above, had built transformers for years at its northern plant. To meet demand it built a new southern plant incorporating the latest manufacturing methods. Management at both plants included Marketing and Engineering functions, and both plants operated as decentralized profit centers. It wasn't long before the southern plant wanted to change designs to suit its needs, independent of the northern plant. This would have resulted in transformers of the same rating and model number, but built at the separate plants, having different designs.

This could have led to customers insisting on buying transformers from one plant or the other, resulting in inventory, pricing and delivery problems. Also the problem of supplying spare parts for ostensibly the same transformer would have become a nightmare.

Obviously this was an impossible situation and product planning (with engineering control of documentation) had to be reasserted at the businesses' headquarters. A single product of uniformly high quality was more important to the business than any benefits derived from competition between the two plants.

Section Four

Operations

With a strong Operations VP in place (responsible for manufacturing and engineering) it should be possible for the CEO to concentrate on strategic planning, organization and manpower development, and shareholder and investor relations, while monitoring and measuring the performance of operations and marketing.

During the early portion of the growth stage the CEO will need to be certain that the systems, procedures and measurements, initiated during the takeoff stage, are completely implemented. The CEO must have the means for measuring performance and exercising control.

Keep crises manageable.

Once assured that the necessary measurements and systems are in place, the CEO should devote sufficient time monitoring operations to keep his fingers on the pulse. The purpose of monitoring is not only to measure the performance of the Operations VP and his direct reports, but to identify emerging problems. The CEO is the one person in the organization who can view the total company, and see it in the context of his vision for the company.

During the growth stage, operations will constantly be on the verge of being overwhelmed. Hiring and assimilating an additional 200 or 300 new employees each year, adding equipment and space, developing suppliers who can provide the increased material requirements, maintaining quality, and the hundreds of details associated with 25% and 50% growth rates, are major undertakings that can challenge the best of operations.

Monitoring doesn't imply looking over the shoulder of the Operations VP and second guessing every move. It also doesn't mean going around the Operations VP and issuing instructions to people in the organization. The CEO should attempt to search for problems that the Operations VP may not recognize due to his intimate involvement with myriad day to day activities, and where those problems suggest an impending crisis.

The CEO's objective is to keep all crises manageable, and not allow them to get out of control.

As a part of the monitoring process, the CEO should allocate some of his time to talk with as many people in the organization as possible. He should avail himself of every such opportunity and build devices into his schedule that will bring him into contact with people. At the same time, the CEO must work through the organization or there will be chaos and demoralization.

One device used by a successful manager was to park his car at the rear of the plant. This required him to walk through the factory where he could stop and talk with employees. Another way to assure contact is to schedule meetings with customers, but to meet in advance with the salesman responsible for the customer and not only with the sales manager or Marketing VP; leaving sufficient time to discuss other matters besides the customer. When multiple shifts are involved, the CEO should occasionally visit late at night or early in the morning. Second and third shifts are traditionally the most difficult to manage, and the Operations VP should visit them on a regular basis. Visits by the CEO make everyone aware of his interest; and the CEO is likely to observe situations worthy of discussion with the Operations VP. When operations are scattered around the country, such as in service businesses, the CEO should routinely make unannounced visits to remote operations.

Whatever his approach, the CEO must learn how to meet with people at all levels of the organization, without usurping the authority of managers or causing managers and supervisors to feel threatened.

Maintaining contact with people in an organization of a thousand or more people is difficult, and may not seem productive since only a few people can be reached. When people believe that the CEO is truly interested in them, as well as in the company, they will want to do their best work. It is also surprizing what the CEO can learn from people who are interested in doing their best. An experienced CEO can learn a great deal by merely walking through an area, whether it is an office or a factory. A cursory understanding of work sampling (see appendix) can provide a statistically valid legitimacy to his observations.

These observations also can be used to demonstrate the CEO's interest in safety and quality. All accidents should be thoroughly investigated by the Operations VP and his staff, with a copy of the accident report sent to the CEO. If the CEO goes to an accident site and discusses the accident with the employees he will earn their respect, gain some insights into employee attitudes toward safety, and be in a better position to influence management and employee attitudes.

Similarly, when the CEO discusses a customer complaint with employees involved with the problem, he demonstrates his interest in quality and gains additional insights into factors that affect quality. Employee attitudes play an important role in safety and quality and the CEO can have a positive impact on those attitudes.

One aspect of the monitoring process is that the CEO should always be looking for ways in which operations can be improved. The CEO should sense how much improvement is possible, and constantly stretch the organization to do better without pushing too hard.

Measuring direct labor.

Another operating decision that must be confronted during the growth stage (and possibly even the takeoff stage), is whether to pay direct labor on the basis of day work or incentive. Day work can either be measured or unmeasured. Measured daywork requires that time standards be established for each operation with employee performance measured and compared to the standard. With measured day work, if, after a reasonable period and after receiving proper training, an employee fails to meet the standard he is let go or reassigned.

The CEO should participate in the decision of which payment system to use. Unmeasured daywork systems make it very difficult to know with any degree of certainty whether employees are achieving acceptable levels of productivity. Measured daywork systems allow management to know when employees meet standard productivity levels, while incentive systems pay the employee a premium for exceeding standard productivity levels.

The unmeasured daywork system places a premium on the quality of supervision. Employee productivity depends entirely on motivation, training and leadership.

Both the measured daywork and incentive systems are expensive to install and must be maintained, otherwise they lose complete meaning over time as methods change.

The CEO should be certain that the benefits to be derived from either a measured daywork or incentive system are worth the costs. He should not agree to a measured daywork or incentive system if he and operating management, are not willing to commit to incurring the cost of maintaining the system.

ACTIONS TO CONSIDER TAKING.

1. Assure integration within the organization.

Manufacturing, engineering, marketing and finance managers should be brought together to be certain they are aware of each others problems, and how the other persons problems impact their function. The CEO needs to be certain that the production and marketing plans mesh, and don't get out of balance. Announcing the availability of a new model or service will prove counter productive if operations is unable to deliver as scheduled. Marketing may be upset, but it may be better to delay introduction until the customer can be assured of delivery. New programs being developed by various components of an organization that affect other functions, should be reviewed at a joint information meeting.

2. Analyze operations monthly.

The Chief Financial Officer should be required to analyze current month's operations and comment on all variances and trends that are likely to have an important impact on the company. The CFO should be expected to highlight all negative variances so that they are not accidentally overlooked. This analysis should be written and then reviewed with the CEO and function vice presidents in a joint meeting where the implications of the report can be thoroughly discussed.

As with marketing, the CEO should insist that reports on key result measurements be on his desk at the close of each month. Refer to figure 11 for a list of operating measurements.

The CEO should give serious consideration to holding monthly staff meetings with his direct reports. It can be at these meetings that the CFO reports on his monthly analysis of operations. Staff meetings also can provide an opportunity for functions to report on programs that are of interest to the others.

They also provide the CEO with an opportunity to develop teamwork, and to build close personal relationships between all members of his immediate staff. He may want to consider social events in conjunction with these meetings: Or to invite speakers having unique views on management or the industry in which the company participates.

As the number of employees increases, it will become difficult for the CEO to meet with all employees on the same basis as he did during the start up and takeoff stages. By building a strong team among those who report directly to him and fostering communications between functions, the CEO can expect that the feelings of team spirit, trust and cooperation will permeate the organization.

3. Keep problems from accumulating.

Problems don't go away, they just pile up. A deadly management sin is to allow problems to remain unresolved. It's up to the CEO to be certain this doesn't happen.

A single problem, no matter how onerous, can be addressed in an orderly manner with adequate resources brought to bear on the problem. When problems are allowed to accumulate they develop into crises where resources are stretched thin and solutions become more intractable.

Section Five

People

During the growth stage, the people issues with which the CEO will be most concerned, are communications, organization and manpower development.

ACTIONS TO CONSIDER TAKING.

1. Implement six step communications program.

With growth in the number of employees accelerating, it will be impossible for the CEO to hold the person to person meetings on which he has previously relied. With a thousand or more employees the CEO must focus his team building efforts on his immediate direct reports, coupled with personal contacts at the next organization layer. This requires involvement with around one hundred employees.

The CEO will continue to contact others, by stopping to talk with employees on the factory floor and elsewhere, but these will primarily be information gathering sessions and a means for establishing credibility in the CEO's interest in people. These individual meetings will not provide the best forum for the CEO to communicate his ideas and vision, explain his actions or the company's progress, or the importance of employee actions regarding quality or other critical performance areas. Another means of communication is needed for these purposes.

The CEO should report periodically to employees on the company's progress and on problems confronting the company, and, if possible, provide a means for employees to question him. If nearly all employees are located in the same city, a local hall or theater can be rented for this purpose. If employees are scattered around the country (or world), a video tape can be made of the meeting held at the home location and distributed for others to see at local meetings conducted by local management.

A traditional method for communicating with employees is through a company newspaper. Each edition of a newspaper can contain a message from the CEO. This is still a good idea and can be done at a reasonable cost. One part time editor, using a $10,000 investment in desk top publishing can publish a monthly newspaper. A more expensive approach was taken by a business with 4000 employees. This company used a professional printer to publish an eight page full sized newspaper four times a year, at a cost of around $200,000. The major drawbacks to a newspaper are that it doesn't allow for a dialogue with the CEO and is far less personal than face to face communications.

Another facet of communications with which the CEO must deal, is the amount of information to give employees. Financial data of large companies is so encompassing that it is difficult for employees to see how the data relates to them, personally. For financial information to be meaningful to employees, large companies would have to break their financial reporting down by unit; which may not even be practical. Large companies have usually resisted this due to cost, and to concern that accidental release of detailed financial information could have strategic value to competitors and investors.

Financial information in the hands of knowledgeable employees can increase employee awareness of the importance of their actions. Giving financial reports to employees also requires managers to explain the reports since most new employees won't understand them. This can improve the dialogue between manager and employee. An awareness and understanding of how each person affects monthly financial results, should enhance the building of a team and gain employee participation in solving difficult problems.

The CEO should balance these conflicting concerns and arrive at an approach that gives employees as much information as possible.

When there are thousands of employees in the company, the CEO's communication strategy boils down to six steps.

(a) Personal team building with his direct reports.

(b) Exerting personal influence through direct contacts with the next layer in the organization: at meetings and during day to day contacts. (The next layer is the layer of people reporting to those who report directly to the CEO.)

(c) Random personal contacts with other employees.

(d) Structured communications, such as video tapes of meetings and a company newspaper.

(e) Providing timely and meaningful information to all employees.

(f) Demonstrating through personal conduct; that he is competent, that he practices what he preaches, has a genuine interest in people, has a vision for the business that commands respect, and that he is worthy of peoples' trust.

2. Select the best organization structure for growth.

The CEO must select the organization structure that he believes best suits the company during the growth stage. There are three basic structures from which to choose.

(1) Traditional line and staff.

(2) Functional versus decentralized P&L centers.

(3) Matrix.

The traditional line and staff places considerable influence in the hands of staff, premised on the staffs "authority of knowledge". The major drawbacks to corporate staffs (proven repeatedly) are that they tend to grow and perpetuate themselves, and that they detract from the operating managers ability to act in a timely and forceful manner. The major advantage of a staff is its ability to study issues objectively, without the pressure of daily operations. Some staff is almost inescapable, with accounting and strategic planning common staff activities.

The CEO should be careful to limit the staffs role to evaluating issues for the CEO and operating management, and assure that the staff does not unduly influence operating decisions. If the CEO doesn't act forcefully in this regard the staff will expand and the company's decision making process will be victimized by a bureaucratic review process. Managerial sclerosis will set in.

The functional organization places sole responsibility for profit and loss in the hands of the CEO. The decentralized organization establishes separate profit and loss centers with General Managers in charge of each, with the CEO retaining overall profit and loss responsibility. In a decentralized organization the manufacturing, engineering, finance and marketing functions are assigned to each decentralized P&L center, although there are organization structures where marketing (or another function) is a pooled resource.

Single line product companies are typically organized along functional lines. It is difficult to see, for example, how a manufacturer of aircraft jet engines could have a decentralized organization, with independent P&L centers. Blades and vanes couldn't very well be a profit center selling to a compressor assembly P&L center, and so on. It might be possible to establish P&L centers for large and small aircraft jet engines, although even here the common technology and markets doesn't make this a very attractive choice. (Program management is probably a better alternative.)

Automobile companies are fundamentally single product line companies, but have chosen to segment their markets by type of customer, establishing separate divisions for this purpose; with each division having profit and loss responsibility.

Multiproduct line companies may elect to establish separate profit and loss centers for each product line. General Electric, Westinghouse Electric, and United Technologies are examples.

Service businesses should, on the other hand, give careful consideration to adopting a decentralized organization structure, especially when the business is geographically dispersed. A service business with cornerstone operations in 15 major cities, could easily have the manager of each territory, formed around the cornerstone operations, be responsible for profitability.

For example, the average transaction of a product service business that repairs and maintains computers and communication equipment is only a few hundred dollars. Each transaction is usually unique, with separate prices having to be developed for each transaction. A $50 million product service business could easily have 2000 separate and unique transactions each week. A typical customer for this business would generate $10,000 in sales. A large customer would generate sales of $50,000. This type of business could easily have three thousand customers. Product density and the geographic distribution of products and customers will vary between the fifteen territories. With such diversity it is extremely difficult for the CEO (or a single Operations VP) to make intelligent decisions concerning day to day operations for each service territory. Decentralized decision making and responsiveness to customer needs are important considerations for a service business of this type.

A service business such as Federal Express is more analogous to a single line product company and probably would find decentralized profit centers inappropriate. A prerequisite for decentralized profit centers, is for the General Manager to have the freedom to set most prices. He may be restricted from setting prices for a few items. If he lacks pricing authority he is managing a cost center, not a profit center. Federal Express and UPS need a standard pricing formula for all their customers, unless volume or other factors result in discounts. Presumably any such discounts would be centrally approved.

Some advantages of a decentralized organization structure include:

(a) Placing decision making authority close to the customer to better respond to the customers' needs.

(b) Developing managers who are focused on profitability.

(c) Providing the flexibility that permits General Managers to focus on customers and services that are most profitable.

The major disadvantages of a decentralized organization structure include:

(a) Higher cost than a functional organization, caused by the extra layer of General Managers, each having functional managers reporting to them.

(b) The difficulty of maintaining a common focus for the business so that the company's efforts aren't fragmented and its resources dissipated.

The matrix type of organization structure has functional (or operating) management coexisting with program management. Figures 23 and 24 illustrate two types of matrix organizations.

In the product business (Figure 23) functional management (engineering, manufacturing, etc.) is responsible for the management of resources; men, plant, and equipment. The program managers are responsible for having the functional managers allocate resources to their programs, to achieve on time completion of their programs. This type of approach is widely used in the defense industry.

In the service business (Figure 24) operating management is responsible for day to day operations, while program managers are responsible for developing and introducing new service offerings. This separates short range from longer range work.

For example, the program manager is assigned responsibility for developing a new service offering, such as maintenance and repair service for PBX (Private Branch Telephone exchange) phone equipment. Previously the business had provided maintenance, repair and installation services for data communications equipment.

The program manager would develop the marketing strategy, identify the technical resources (people, tools and equipment) and the parts inventory required to support the new PBX service. He would assure proper implementation of the new service by having operating management train the necessary people, stock the needed parts, and initiate the needed sales effort.

A matrix organization is an effective approach to managing a diversification strategy for a service business and allows the CEO to retain control over how the company will diversify. Without such an approach the decentralized operating departments are likely to pursue separate strategies that fragment the company's efforts.

MATRIX ORGANIZATION FOR A PRODUCT BUSINESS				
Product management. (1)	Functional management. (2)			
	Engineering	Manufacturing	Marketing	Finance
Program manager, product line A.				
Program manager, product line B.				
Program manager, product line C.				
Program manager, product line D.				

Figure 23

Notes to figure 23:

1. Program managers are responsible for having resources allocated to their programs to meet program schedules.

2. Function management responsible for day to day management and supervision of resources.

MATRIX ORGANIZATION FOR A SERVICE BUSINESS				
Product management.	Functional management.			
	P&L Center #1	P&L Center #2	P&L Center #3	P&L Center #4
Program manager, service A.				
Program manager, service B.				
Program manager, service C.				
Program manager, service D.				

Figure 24

Notes to figure 24:

1. Program managers are responsible for developing and introducing new service offerings, for book prices and program profitability.

2. Function management responsible for day to day operations and profitability.

These represent some alternative organization structures from which the CEO must choose. In the final analysis the CEO must decide which organization structure will be best for the company. The board of directors also will probably be interested in this issue and the CEO should be ready to explain his decision and obtain the board's agreement.

3. Rely on four actions to develop people.

Among the CEO's most important responsibilities is the development of people at all levels of the organization. The company cannot grow unless there is a steady supply of trained workers, supervisors, and managers.

The best way to attract good people is for the company to become known as a good place to work, not because it pays high wages, but because it offers opportunities for growth and advancement. This halo effect will be the by-product of an effective manpower development program.

The primary factors contributing to the successful development of people are: (1) To provide each employee with a meaningful job, (2) To reward excellent performance, (3) To provide opportunities for learning, (4) To demonstrate that advancement and financial rewards are the results of good performance.

The only person who can assure the existence of these conditions is the CEO. The magnitude of the task, when thousands of employees are involved, requires that the CEO establish a process involving the entire management team. The natural inclination is to hire a Manager of Employee Relations, or Manager of Personnel, or Manager of Training and Manpower Development.

Although the CEO will need help administering the training and development process, he should resist the temptation of turning the manpower development process over to a "professional". The last thing the CEO wants is for a third party to interject himself between the CEO (and other managers) and the employee. Each manager should make judgements about employees who report directly to them and to their immediate subordinates (one over one). This is better than allowing a "professional" to gather information on employees and then interject his judgement on the employees' managerial potential and worth to the company. No matter how good the "professional" manpower person, the fact remains that he has probably never run a business, dealt with customers or met a payroll. He will be a theoretician who can, at best, provide some insight into what motivates a particular individual.

An effective personnel development program can be divided into two parts. The first will be highly structured and consist of the following seven elements.

(a) Each year every employee should update his personal work history record (resume), including any training courses he has taken. A photo should be attached, if possible.

(b) A simple job description should be prepared for every position other than direct labor. It should include the type of experience and training normally required to do the job successfully, and the criteria on which performance will be measured. Figure 25 illustrates a job description form, which can also be used for the annual performance appraisal. Combining the job description and appraisal documents helps assure that job descriptions are kept current while easing the administrative burden.

(c) Every employee's performance should be evaluated by his immediate manager at least once each year, and then reviewed and approved by the next higher manager. After completing the one over one review the performance appraisal should be reviewed with the employee. Performance appraisals of hourly employees also should be done unless it is precluded by contract.

The appraisal form should be kept simple and should stress job performance, with a minimum of attention placed on traits. A single space to comment on any unusually good or bad trait is sufficient. Each employee should sign the appraisal and comment on it if he or she is in disagreement with some aspect of the appraisal.

(d) Each employee should be advised of the training he should take to help qualify for positions in which he is interested. This should be a part of the review procedure.

(e) Copies of the work history, job description and current performance appraisal of every employee in a manager's organization should be given to the manager. While the company is in the growth stage the CEO should receive copies for every employee in the company.

(f) A list of technical and non-technical courses should be compiled for the company. The list can be generated by identifying the skills and attributes required for each job in the company, and by then working with local colleges, high schools, and correspondence schools, to identify applicable courses. The employee would be reimbursed for the cost of each course he successfully passes.

In house training classes can be established for technical training not otherwise available, or to cover material that is unique to the company.

The second part of the personnel development program would involve the personal participation of every manager and the CEO. Each manager would meet with his direct reports and collectively review the performance and potential of every employee in the managers' organization, other than his direct reports. The performance and potential of each employee reporting to the managers' direct reports (one over one) should be discussed. Outstanding employees further down the organization should be identified.

For example, the manager of each employee would state how long the employee had been on the job, what his performance had been (satisfactory, outstanding, etc.), whether the employee is ready for promotion, whether the employee has unusually strong or weak traits, whether the employee should be considered for transfer to a different part of the organization for broadening, and whether there is some unusual training that the employee should take that wouldn't have been covered during the employee appraisal routine. Other managers would comment on the employee if they had worked with him during the preceding year.

The senior manager would note any comments on a copy of the employee's work history for later reference and for use at the manpower review that his manager would hold. This type of review will require two full days for each organization layer.

Many benefits should be derived from these review meetings. First, each manager should compile a list of people whom he would recommend as candidates for his job, the job of others at the same organization level and for those who report directly to him. Second, the training and development needs of employees can be revised based on these discussions. Third, negative feedback concerning an employee can be noted and arrangements made for the manager or supervisor to counsel the employee. Fourth, misunderstandings that could derail an employee's career can be addressed and resolved.

Combined Job Description and Appraisal Form
(Maintain on personal computer to facilitate annual update.)

Title: Manager Manufacturing Engineering.

Responsibilities: Manage manufacturing Engineers assigned to him so as to identify and develop the best processes, methods, tooling, equipment and factory layouts and thereby achieve the lowest possible manufacturing costs while maintaining the highest standard of quality. Manage the company's hazardous waste program. Complete all assigned projects on time. Staff his organization with the best qualified people and develop them so that they maintain state of the art capabilities and become qualified for advancement.

Qualifications: Should have five years experience as a manufacturing engineer, preferably involved with the manufacture of electronic products. Must be a college graduate with a BS, BSEE, BSME or Industrial Engineering degree.

Performance criteria for 1988:
1. Complete project "A" by June 1, within the established budget.
2. Debug and make operational new coating process, achieving acceptable quality on 99.5% of all parts by March 15.
3. Complete the plant layout for new product to be introduced in the second quarter, by September 1 and complete the installation of equipment (all currently on order) by August 2.
4. Identify projects, in conjunction with shop operations, that will result in cost improvements of $750,000: Complete these projects by 31 December.
5. Arrange for the proper identification, collection and disposal of all hazardous waste generated by the company, and proper handling and storage of hazardous materials used by the company, in a way that keeps the company from being cited for violations.
6. Provide challenging assignments for employees, encourage employee development and maintain a high level of enthusiasm in the Manufacturing Engineering organization.
7. Operate the organization within the established budget.
(Other performance criteria as appropriate.)

Performance criteria established with employee on: Jan. 15
Signed: (J. Brighton) Manufacturing VP.

(Employee: R. Campbell) Mgr. Manufacturing Engineering.

Figure 25 (Front side)

Performance Appraisal:
Criteria   Rating   Comments
 #   O   FS LS U _____

1. _____
2. _____
3. _____
4. _____
5. _____
6. _____
7. _____

_____
_____
_____
_____
_____

Overall performance was:_____

Other comments concerning employee performance:

_____
_____
_____
_____

Recommended training:

_____
_____

Reviewed with employee on __ signed: _(manager)_____

Employee comments:

_____
_____

    signed: _(employee)___

Figure 25 (Reverse side)

When an opening exists, the manager responsible for filling the opening should compile a list of candidates, preferably no fewer than four. The proposed candidate slate (together with a brief job description) would be sent to his immediate superior, with a copy to the CEO. Both these managers could make additions or deletions, before approving the list of candidates. If there is disagreement concerning the needs of the position or the qualifications of a candidate, they can be discussed and resolved before the interview process begins. The hiring manager can then proceed with the interviews and fill the job from the slate of approved candidates.

In no way does the candidate selection process detract from the hiring managers ability to hire the best person for the job since he compiled the original candidate slate. The process insures, however, that all the best people are considered for the job since the CEO and the immediate manager can make additions to the candidate slate. The process also helps insure that a crony won't be considered for the job since the hiring manager's boss will have had an opportunity to screen the slate. As a result, every employee will know that the selection process has been thorough and fair.

Under no circumstances should any portion of this part of the process be delegated to an employee relations or management development person.

The manpower development process outlined above represents a major commitment by management. It requires a minimum of paper work and bureaucracy. It places responsibility for success on management - where it belongs. The CEO will need to support this effort and make known his personal commitment to having it succeed.

4. Avoid a bureaucratic manpower organization.

The manpower development process is easily encumbered with frills that, at first blush, seem useful, but develop into a quagmire, where form (and Forms) is more important than substance. A case in point is the use of backup charts, where each manager identifies employees whom he believes are viable replacements for himself and for those reporting to him. These charts are seldom used when it comes time to prepare a candidate slate. Typically, the same people are listed by several managers so that they have been promoted before the backup chart can be used. Finally, someone needs to keep and analyze the backup charts, which interjects an intermediary, in the form of an employee relations or manpower specialist, into the process.

Another example of where form replaces substance is the typical job description, half of which consists of boiler plate. These job descriptions are usually kept on file (in the manpower organization), and are seldom used. Periodically the manpower specialist sends them to managers for updating. This activity is considered a burden by managers since the job descriptions are an adjunct, and not an integral part of the personnel development process.

The objectives of the personnel development process are to identify promotable people, make certain they receive the training and experience needed to qualify them for promotion, and encourage people to enter self development programs that raise the calibre of the entire organization. An effective personnel development program builds esprit de corps. With an effective program everyone knows that opportunities for advancement are available to all, and that the company is staffed by the best people available.

Any activity that obfuscates or complicates the development process should be eliminated, cut out, like the cancer it is.

> The organization should be imbued with the philosophy that the sale is not complete until the customer is satisfied and the cash is in the till.

> Capturing a "share of mind" is especially important to a service business where the customer reacts to a momentary event, such as the failure of a piece of equipment, or the need for temporary secretarial service.

PART FOUR

BEYOND THE GROWTH STAGE

As growth slows the company slips into the mature stage. The company that began as a single product line start up, and then evolved through the takeoff and growth stages without broadening its product line, could find itself in an unenviable position when growth slows.

Professional managers spend a lifetime groping with the problems associated with large mature companies. The entrepreneur needs to be aware of what lies ahead though his company may have just entered the takeoff stage. By looking ahead the entrepreneur turned CEO may avoid some sins that have led to the downfall of other companies. Perhaps it won't be necessary for a professional manager to take over from the entrepreneur.

Section One

Cash

The nasty impact of slow growth.

When the knee of the growth curve is reached and growth slows significantly, the need for cash also will slow. The original products that have sustained a successful company's growth, will no longer require additional cash to support the growth of inventories and receivables.

Recognizing that the company has entered the maturing stage is not necessarily easy. The fact that sales have slowed may merely suggest a slowing in the economy or a temporary breather as customers assimilate what they have already purchased, while preparing for the next wave of buying.

The tendency will be for management to believe that continued growth is possible, and to hang on to this view for an extended period. The CEO must look at the world realistically and make the difficult call whether growth has slowed or merely been temporarily interrupted. This is a gut wrenching decision since to err in either direction can have serious consequences. Continued optimism can result in the postponement of actions crucial to keeping the company profitable. Taking action too soon to restructure can emasculate the company and prevent it from capitalizing on renewed growth.

Another consideration in this scenario is the impact of the investment community, especially if the company is public. Stock analysts will be evaluating the company's growth and may be very quick to call the turn, which can have a negative impact on the company's stock price. How the CEO positions the company in the minds of the investment community can be extremely important.

During the period of uncertainty brought on by slower growth, the prudent CEO will tend to place a freeze on hiring and expenses. He can begin the positioning process (which is also beneficial if sales are down due to a slow economy) without seriously eating into the core strength of the company.

If the company has entered the mature stage, it is at a crossroads; albeit a crossroads that should have been addressed earlier, while the company was still in the growth stage.

The choices are few. New products can be added or new markets found to restimulate growth. Without new products or markets the company can drift along and, if it generates cash, become a cash cow, ripe for takeover. Or eventually just wither away.

Existing products must generate cash.

Regardless of the company's strategy at this juncture, existing products or services need to be viewed as cash generators. If the company opts to restimulate growth, either through the development of new products or acquisitions (or another form of diversification), it will need cash to carry out the strategy. If the company opts to be sold, a strong cash position will enhance the value of the company. If the company opts to drift, it is going to need the cash to fend off takeovers.

An important characteristic of a mature product (or industry) is that the product often becomes a commodity. As this happens it will become difficult to obtain any price premium, and the price level will tend to decline to a level where the lowest cost producer is marginally profitable.

With the prospect of declining margins, management needs to focus on reducing costs (especially if the company is not the low cost producer). Cash also will be needed, therefore, to invest in a cost reduction program to remain profitable.

The challenge facing the CEO when the company matures, is to reposition marketing and operations so that existing products generate as much cash as possible. This may not be easy to do if the company has been geared to growth, with both marketing and operations thinking in terms of growth and expansion. In fact, the probability is that the organization already has too many employees, hired in anticipation of continued growth.

ACTIONS TO CONSIDER TAKING.

1. Downsizing the organization.

In as far as existing products are concerned, the organization should be examined to determine where reductions can be made. Each component should be asked to reduce the number of people so that organization size reflects physical sales volume and productivity improvements.

Sales may be increasing in current dollars, merely reflecting inflation. To arrive at manpower budgets, sales must be adjusted to represent physical volume as closely as possible. The simplest approach is to recast sales in constant dollars, using an appropriate base year, and to compare organization size against sales in constant dollars.

Even where physical sales volume stays constant, the organization must be challenged to reduce people through productivity improvements and through restructuring of the organization.

Annual wage and salary increases are frequently going to offset savings from manpower reductions and cause a net increase in compensation costs. This may literally force the company to budget a precise amount for wage and salary increases, distributing it across the organization based on performance. Hourly wage increases cannot exceed productivity improvements without negatively affecting the company.

A service business with high labor content (such as a product service business) should be careful how it establishes manpower reduction targets, since people who perform the service (direct labor) are analogous to "product" in a manufacturing company. Any increase in real volume, as opposed to sales increases due to inflation, will be accompanied by an increase in people to do the work. If real volume remains constant, manpower (direct labor as opposed to overhead) reductions can only come from productivity improvements. Assuming the work force is already properly motivated, productivity improvements can only be achieved through changes in methods or procedures. These changes can be more difficult to achieve than in a manufacturing company, where the work tends to be better defined and more repetitious.

Another major problem in establishing manpower reduction targets for a service business is in measuring physical volume. Constant dollar sales could provide a totally erroneous measure of physical volume. Product mix can be extremely difficult to establish in a service business, with changes in product mix almost impossible to quantify. If product mix changes substantially, sales in constant dollars alone cannot be used to determine physical volume. It is much easier for a manufacturing company to quantify changes in product mix than for a labor intensive service business. A labor intensive service business must work harder at productivity improvements since compensation costs represent a larger percentage of total costs.

Every business can reduce overhead by restructuring the organization and eliminating staff positions performing non-essential tasks.

2. Beef up cost improvement efforts.

In addition to actions aimed at reducing the number of employees, a planned approach needs to be developed for reducing other costs. The company should already have an established cost reduction program rewarding employees for their contributions in this area, but it often only chips away at costs. In addition to these cost reduction actions, the company needs an organized approach to identifying the areas of greatest opportunity.

Redefining the organization's goals from those associated with growth, to goals that are appropriate to the management of a slow growth business, is both a challenge and an opportunity. The challenge comes from people not wanting to change or accept that the nature of the business has changed. The opportunity derives from being able to relook at every facet of the business from a new perspective: It permits rethinking established views.

For example, if the business is no longer growing, the need for previously planned expansions of sales offices may no longer exist. It also may be possible to consolidate existing sales offices. These alternatives probably would not have been examined if the direction of the business had not been redefined.

The CEO must, therefore, be certain that everyone understands and accepts the new direction. It will be to his advantage to participate in defining the cost improvement program and identifying areas of greatest opportunity. It may even be necessary for him to ask the hard questions initially; or at least until others accept the new direction and begin to participate. Opportunities for savings will vary from company to company, but asking tough questions can help the organization focus on the new strategy. "How can we consolidate office space to reduce our rents?", or "Can we sell excess space?", or "Can we restructure our product line to reduce the number of models to save on inventory and other costs"? may be appropriate. Questions such as, "How many phone extensions and features can we eliminate to reduce rental and service costs?", or "How can we reduce travel and entertainment expenses by 30%?", can help establish the tone for the new direction.

Material costs need to be quantified and potential savings identified. Distribution costs need to be studied for possible savings.

Excesses, inefficiencies and carelessness are bound to have proliferated in any company that has grown rapidly. A profitable, growing company will find that success hides many sins. All overhead expenses need to be reexamined to identify cost reduction opportunities. Expenses to be studied include power consumption, maintenance costs, shipping costs, phone bills, and overnight courier services.

3. Avoid business as usual.

The CEO needs to get the message across that times have changed. The new reality is that the company is not growing and that it must conduct itself accordingly. To enlist everyone's support for the new direction requires leadership on the part of management. Management must make it abundantly clear they aren't conducting business as usual. The frills must go.

Section Two

Strategy

Learning from Federal Express and UPS.

The on-going battle between Federal Express and UPS is going to be very interesting to watch, with both companies competing in maturing markets. Federal express has been the leader in the overnight delivery market while UPS has dominated the package delivery market.

Federal Express identified the need for overnight delivery and literally created the market for their service with an entrepreneurial and innovative style. UPS dominated the package delivery market, with a stuffy but very efficient management style.

On the one hand Federal Express priced its services based on value added, with value being derived from the importance customers assign to on time overnight delivery. UPS, on the other hand, had cost leadership in its market and priced accordingly.

The overnight delivery market has not only become saturated, but it has become susceptible to technological change. The inevitable emergence of FAX could even result in the overnight delivery market declining in size.

Federal Express used technological and regulatory change to carve out its market while UPS rested on its laurels, but both may find the market again affected by the change brought about by FAX.

One issue is whether Federal Express can continue to obtain higher prices based on value added or whether pricing will gravitate lower where the product becomes marginally profitable to the low cost producer.

Federal Express appears to have embraced a service strategy by investing in technology that allows them to guarantee overnight delivery while also responding immediately to customer calls for service. They have also moved into package delivery in competition with UPS. UPS appears to have countered with a cost leadership strategy while also investing in the technology that guarantees overnight delivery, but perhaps without the flexibility of Federal Express. UPS has used its size and large cash flow to enter the overnight delivery market aggressively. It is surprising they didn't adopt a preemptive strategy by entering the market sooner, when Federal Express was less able to finance growth.

It is interesting to examine Federal Express' recent strategy where they recognized the threat from FAX and perceived an opportunity to expand into the package delivery market. ZAP mail attacked the FAX threat head on, but ultimately failed after incurring large losses. The failure of ZAP mail was partly attributed to technological problems, though it is difficult to see how ZAP mail could ever have been a success competing with FAX. FAX machines will be in nearly every office in the industrialized free world in the next few years, negating the need for ZAP mail.

The confrontation with UPS also raises the question whether Federal Express should have attempted a strategy that was an end run around UPS (and possibly also FAX). Any gains by Federal Express in the package market had to come at the expense of UPS, threatening UPS's market share. This may have prompted a more vigorous response from UPS than might otherwise have been the case, which now threatens Federal Expresses share of the overnight delivery market.

An end run strategy could have focused on developing new overnight delivery markets (other than documents), thereby enlarging the market and achieving growth in this manner. Overnight delivery of product samples in the rag trade, or spare parts for manufacturers or service companies, or medical samples, or valuables (since they could be tracked and accounted for), are possible ways in which the overnight delivery market could have been expanded without directly challenging UPS. A more timely international strategy, rather than wasting time on ZAP mail, could also have been an end run around UPS.

Without inside information this is merely speculation, but illustrates how difficult it is to arrive at an effective strategy when the product reaches maturity and the company's growth starts to slow. Federal Express is innovative, smart, successful, and financially sound; but even they are having difficulties.

ACTIONS TO CONSIDER TAKING.

1. Preserve positive cash flow, or prepare to leave.

Confronted with a narrow product line that is maturing the CEO needs to adopt a two pronged strategy. The initial phase of the strategy will be to maximize cash flow from existing products, while the second phase focuses on diversification to revitalize growth. Maintaining a strong balance sheet and remaining profitable with a positive cash flow, is an overriding objective of any strategy developed at this stage.

The CEO must take whatever steps are necessary to maintain profitability and a positive cash flow. Virtually nothing is possible without a positive cash flow.

2. Rethink the Marketing strategy for existing products.

The cost reduction aspects of this strategy have already been discussed. Actions taken by marketing, involving pricing, product line configuration, distribution, and the concentration of sales effort are the other key ingredients in generating cash from existing products.

Before marketing can develop its plans it needs to know whether the company's strategy is to maintain market share. If the company has a large market share of roughly 30% or more, and its nearest competitor has a significantly smaller share of perhaps less than 15%, the company probably can assume that it has cost leadership. It should make an effort to confirm this since pricing and other actions depend on whether the company has significant cost leadership. If the company's market share position is reversed, it probably can assume that it does not have cost leadership.

If the market is fragmented with many companies having a small share, and with no one having a major share, cost leadership could be hard to establish. If the company could establish significant cost leadership in a fragmented market it might adopt an aggressive pricing strategy to reestablish growth by capturing market share and driving others from the market. The reverse also could happen if the company's cost structure was appreciably higher than that of the low cost producer. In a fragmented market it is unlikely that anyone has significant cost leadership, although it is important to confirm that this is correct.

If the company's strategy is to maintain market share it must be prepared to meet lower prices and give up margin. A limit should be established on how much margin the company is willing to forego or identify where it is willing to give up share and where it will keep share.

On the other hand if the company's strategy is to maintain its margins at the expense of market share, it needs to define where or to what extent it is willing to do so.

The CEO will need to establish these guidelines for marketing and monitor how the marketing strategy affects margins and market share, and whether marketing actions are maximizing cash generation.

3. Five ways to establish a new growth strategy.

There are essentially five ways in which to establish a new growth strategy, assuming the availability of cash and a strong balance sheet.

(a) Develop new applications for the product, and thereby <u>expand the market</u> to achieve growth.

(b) <u>Develop new and different products,</u> either internally through R&D or by buying product rights.

(c) <u>Enter new markets.</u> This could include international markets or markets opened by acquiring a company, or a division from another company.

(d) <u>Capture market share</u> through aggressive pricing or, if possible, through product differentiation.

(e) <u>Sell the existing business</u> and use the proceeds to acquire new businesses.

The last alternative is a draconian measure but could be the best choice if the company has a small market share. It may not be a viable alternative unless the company's product line or engineering or manufacturing capabilities complement those of a competitor who is interested in such an acquisition. General Electric's sale of the computer business to help finance the jet engine and other businesses is an example of such a strategy.

Pricing aggressively to capture market share is only possible if the company has a distinct cost advantage or can differentiate its product in an important way. It is a high risk strategy since competition will try to meet the lower price level, so long as they can remain solvent. Even if a competitor enters bankruptcy there is no guarantee that it won't emerge from bankruptcy in a strong financial position, shed of a major part of its debt.

Achieving meaningful product differentiation this late in the product life cycle is also unlikely, although still possible. Product differentiation should have been a major part of the company's original growth strategy.

A significant technological breakthrough can result in new models of an existing product that are significantly superior in one or more attributes, which can lead to product differentiation and major gains in market share

The most likely alternatives for revitalizing growth, therefore, are the first three. Again, the first two alternatives should have been made a part of the company's strategy during the growth stage.

Clearly, a strong balance sheet and good cash flow from the existing product lines are essential to these strategic alternatives.

It is worth noting that alternative (e) also may be an excellent strategy for a start up company or a company in the takeoff stage, where its sales have flattened though the industry is growing rapidly. This could be the case when a few large companies dominate the industry and a start up introduces important new technology without the marketing clout to take significant share away from the dominant players.

The PBX (telephone equipment) market is an excellent example of where this has recently occurred. In the early 1980's AT&T and Northern Telecom were the major producers of PBX telephone switching systems. Rolm, Mitel, Intecom and others developed new PBX's based on computers and digital technologies, that were faster and offered many new and important features unavailable with existing PBX's. Among these new features was the PBX's ability to connect directly to computers and other equipment, such as printers, to form an inexpensive local area network (LAN) and provide integrated voice and data communications.

Rolm, as the early developer of the computer based digital PBX, was the most successful of the new entrants. Mitel was originally successful with small units but ran into serious problems in trying to develop larger PBX's that were capable of handling two thousand or more phones.

Intecom, a later entrant, introduced technology that was ahead of both Rolm and Mitel. None of these companies (or the many other less successful entrants or GTE and Siemens who are also still active participants in the market) were able to fully penetrate the market due to AT&T's and Northern Telecom's dominant market positions, though Rolm did reasonably well in this respect.

In the final analysis Rolm was purchased by IBM and then later sold to a European multinational telecommunications company. Intecom was purchased by Wang and later sold to Matra a french communications company. And Mitel was purchased by British Telecom.

None of these innovative start-up companies with superior technology could make it on their own against entrenched competition.

Section Three

Marketing

Price for market share or fatter margins.

The CEO needs to decide whether the company's cash generation strategy, for its existing product lines in a mature market, is best achieved by maintaining market share or maintaining margins.

The tactical situation confronting marketing in a mature market will be similar to one of those depicted in Figures 27 through 29 where there are either highly concentrated markets with only a few competitors, or moderately concentrated markets with a reasonable number of competitors, or fragmented markets with many competitors. (Figure 26 describes the format used in these figures.) In each of these market structures there may or may not be a dominant competitor with the largest share of the market.

Scenario 1A: Highly concentrated market with dominant company.

Scenario 2A: Moderately concentrated market with dominant company.

Scenario 3A: Fragmented market with dominant company.

Scenario 1B: Highly concentrated market and no dominant company.

Scenario 2B: Moderately concentrated market and no dominant company.

Scenario 3B: Fragmented market and no dominant company.

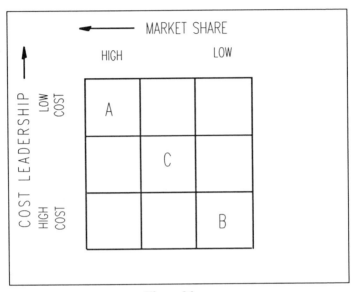

Figure 26

Notes for figure 26:

The above format is used in figures 27 through 29. Company "A", positioned at the upper left has a very high market share and a very strong cost leadership position. Company "B" has very high costs and a very low market share. Other companies will be positioned on the grid depending on their market share and costs. Company "C" has average costs and a moderately strong market share. In this example company "A" holds a dominant position, especially with respect to company "B".

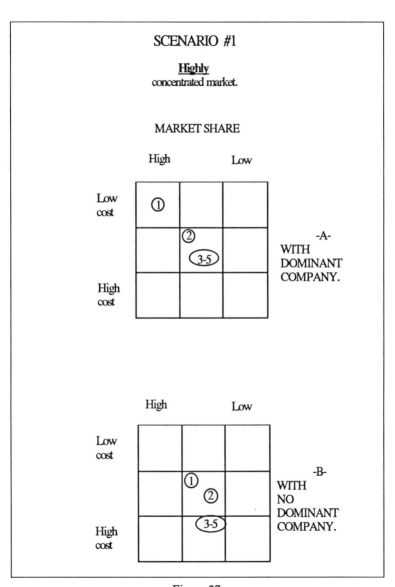

Figure 27

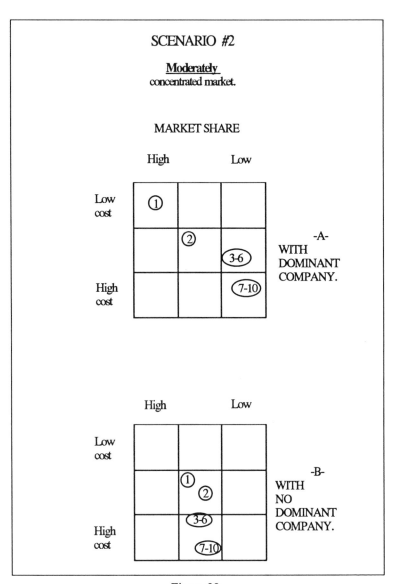

Figure 28

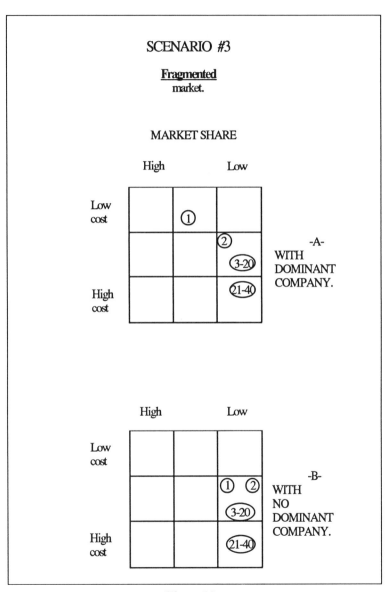

Figure 29

In these figures it is assumed that the dominant company also has significant cost leadership. This may not always be the case. For example, a service company may have achieved its leadership position as the result of high quality service.

Marketing must make key decisions relating to:

(a) Pricing.

(b) Distribution.

(c) Product line configuration.

(d) Concentration of sales effort.

(e) Product differentiation

Product line configuration and concentration of sales effort are primarily functions of market segmentation, either segmenting the market by product line or by type of customer.

Product differentiation of a mature product could include styling.

Since the marketing strategy will be designed to support the company strategy of maximizing income (cash flow) from existing products, it is necessary to examine the pricing alternatives available to marketing under the six basic scenarios depicted in figures 27 through 29.

The company's strategy should call for reducing costs each year by some forecast amount. These cost savings can either be allowed to drop to the bottom line or can be used to reduce prices. If used to reduce prices the price reductions should, (a) result in increased sales and market share since it is assumed that the market is mature and is not growing in real terms or, (b) protect market share by meeting actual or threatened competitive pricing actions.

A simple computer program (see appendix) can show how large the sales increase must be to generate sufficient income to offset a price reduction. Examining the basic scenarios (figures 27 through 29) while referring to the tables in the appendix, can help illustrate which pricing actions are likely to be productive.

Pricing and market concentration.

Attempting to increase market share in a mature market is extremely difficult, especially if the objective is also to increase total income and cash generation.

This is especially true in a highly concentrated "oligopolistic" market (with or without a dominant leader) since each company is watching the actions of the other and can be expected to respond to pricing actions to protect share. Any increase in sales by one company will be at the expense of the others, and will be immediately visible to everyone.

A price decrease would have to generate sufficient additional income to more than offset the price decrease, if the company's objective is to increase income. A 1% across the board price decrease by company #1, must generate the sales shown in Table 2 of appendix, (depending on the market share held by company #1 before the price decrease) to maintain current income dollars. Increased sales by company #1 would result in a corresponding loss of sales by competitors, which, on average, is also shown in Table 2.

The larger the market share held by company #1, the greater must be its increase in sales to offset a 1% price decrease.

Whenever there is a highly concentrated market the resultant loss of sales by competitors would be so severe that they would have to respond by reducing prices to protect their market shares. The same can also be true in a moderately concentrated market. The result would be lower prices and no significant increase in sales for company #1.

Table 2 from appendix, shows that the only possible situation where a price decrease has some chance of increasing sales and total income, is when the market is fragmented and there is no dominant company.

It is also unlikely that a price decrease as small as 1% would result in increased sales, and that decreases on individual models would have to be 5% or more (averaging 1% overall). This means that any price decrease probably would have to be targeted and be part of a market segmentation strategy.

Clearly, the best time to attempt to increase market share with lower prices, is when the market is growing and competitors are not negatively affected by loss of share. They may not even recognize that they are loosing share until it is too late to take effective action.

Another pricing option open to the company is to increase prices, which could result in lost sales and market share and reduced income. If prices can be raised, however, it will result in greater total income and may be worth the risk. Competitors also must raise their prices following your lead, if the price increase is to be successful. Assuming no inflationary pressure, a price increase is most likely to succeed in a highly concentrated market, and has very little chance of succeeding in a fragmented market. Whether it can succeed in a moderately concentrated market is problematical, and depends on prior history. The greater the number of competitors, the less likely a price increase will succeed.

A price increase is more likely to succeed if there is a dominant company in the market, and if the dominant company initiates the price increase. If another company initiates the price increase the dominant company must follow quickly or the increase will not stick.

Selective price increases also can be attempted if it is desired to prune the product line or customer base. Some product models and customers carry a cost penalty and selective price increases can either recover the cost penalty or eliminate the model or customer in question. Before attempting this it is crucial to know how much fixed overhead is liquidated by the incremental sales that would be lost if the increase were not successful.

It has been assumed throughout the previous discussion that any competitive advantages enjoyed by the product (quality, features, etc.) are already reflected in the price (as a price premium), and that increases or decreases in price are from that level. Figures 30 and 31 summarize the appropriateness of price increases or decreases for each market structure.

Responding to price decreases.

In addition to the above, the CEO must decide how the company should respond to price decreases initiated by competitors. The competitor's price decrease can be across the board affecting all models and customers, or it can be selective (reflecting a strategy of product or market segmentation), or it can be targeted at a specific transaction.

With respect to across the board decreases, the company can either follow in order to maintain share at the lower price level, or it can try to maintain higher prices (at least for specific market segments) and lose share in the process. This is similar to the situation outlined earlier, except the company is responding to, rather than initiating the price decrease.

All factors, other than price, may not be equal and it is important to examine them before deciding whether to meet, or partially meet, the lower price. These factors can determine whether the company or its product has competitive advantages that might command a price premium.

(1) Features

(2) Quality (reliability)

(3) Operating cost savings

(4) Service

PRICE INCREASE. (a)			
	SCENARIO #1 Highly concentrated market.	SCENARIO #2 Moderately concentrated market.	SCENARIO #3 Fragmented market.
With dominant company.	May be successful.	Questionable.	High Risk.
With no dominant company.	May be successful. (b)	Very questionable.	High Risk.

Figure 30

PRICE DECREASE. (a)			
	SCENARIO #1 Highly concentrated market.	SCENARIO #2 Moderately concentrated market.	SCENARIO #3 Fragmented market.
With dominant company.	High Risk.	High Risk.	High Risk.
With no dominant company.	High Risk.	High Risk.	Least Risk. (c)

Figure 31

Notes to figures 30 and 31.

(a) Assumes: Mature product or market. No inflationary pressure. Competitive advantages derived from features, quality, etc. already reflected in price.

(b) Dominant firm must follow quickly, otherwise little chance of success.

(c) Best attempted in conjunction with market segmentation strategy.

(5) Brand name

(6) Styling

The CEO must continue to participate in all pricing actions since they can seriously affect income, especially when the product or market is mature. The ability to increase prices in an inflationary environment is even more important since higher prices are often needed to offset higher costs. Getting price increases to stick is often extremely difficult and can lead executives to collude with competitors, which is against the law. The CEO must protect himself and his company from such actions, and he can do this best by retaining control over pricing actions.

ACTIONS TO CONSIDER TAKING.

1. Segment the market to increase profits.

By definition a mature product will tend to become a commodity that is hard to differentiate. As mentioned earlier, a significant technological breakthrough can change this picture and probably the company's strategy. Assuming no such breakthrough is possible, it is up to marketing to analyze the product and market to best position the product to maximize income and cash generation. The product and market analysis should have been started much earlier so that this effort will merely be a continuation of work done during the growth or takeoff stages.

In its simplest form the analysis should identify every attribute of the product and company that is significantly superior or inferior to those of the competition. Similarly customers should be evaluated to find out how important each attribute is to a customer (or group of customers). Customer focus groups and other market research techniques can be used to assure the validity of these evaluations.

Figure 32 depicts a hypothetical analysis of attributes for a single product model, between companies. Figure 33 shows a similar analysis of the importance of the attributes to four customers (or groups of customers). Figure 34 shows a composite evaluation of the company and its competitors for each customer (or customer groups). The composite is arrived at by multiplying the ratings for each attribute by the importance rating for each customer.

This type of evaluation, when done for specific customers, can determine how the sales effort should be focused. For example, product feature "A" and "operating savings" have been determined to be the most important attributes to customer #1. The company's sales force should emphasize product feature "A" (rated superior against competitors #2 and #3), and "operating savings" (rated superior against competitors #1 and #3).

This evaluation also can highlight possible cost improvement opportunities. Product feature "D" is shown to be of least importance to all four customers. This feature is rated as superior for competitor #2. Either competitor #2 needs to sell the customer on the importance of this feature to establish a competitive advantage, or it should consider cutting back on product feature "D" if costs can be reduced.

When customers are grouped by market segment the analysis can help identify opportunities for differentiating the product or for restructuring the product line to increase sales or increase income.

Customers 1 through 4 in figures 33 and 34 could represent a group of customers, rather than single customers.

ANALYSIS OF PRODUCT XYZ.				
ATTRIBUTES.	Company	Competitor #1	Competitor #2	Competitor #3
Feature "A".	3	2	1	1
Feature "B".	3	1	2	1
Feature "C".	2	1	2	1
Feature "D".	1	2	3	1
Quality/Reliability.	3	1	2	1
Operating savings.	3	1	2	1
Service.	3	2	3	1
Brand name.	1	1	1	1
Styling.	1	1	1	1

Figure 32

Figure 32 Scoring:
    Doesn't meet minimum requirements. = 0
    Meets minimum requirements. = 1
    Significantly better than minimum requirements. = 2
    Superior = 4

IMPORTANCE OF ATTRIBUTES TO EACH CUSTOMER				
ATTRIBUTES.	Customer #1	Customer #2	Customer #3	Customer #4
Feature "A".	3	2	2	1
Feature "B".	2	2	2	1
Feature "C".	2	2	2	1
Feature "D".	1	1	1	1
Quality/Reliability.	1	3	2	1
Operating savings.	3	1	1	1
Service.	0	3	1	1
Brand name.	0	0	0	0
Styling.	0	0	0	0

Figure 33

Figure 33 scoring:
Feature has no importance. = 0
Important, but not worth a price premium. 1
Important, worth a small price premium. 2
Extremely important, worth a large premium. 3
Critical. Must have regardless of price. 4

COMPARISON, COMPANY VERSUS COMPETITORS.				
ATTRIBUTES.	Customer #1	Customer #2	Customer #3	Customer #4
Company	32	38	29	18
Competitor #1	16	20	15	10
Competitor #2	22	30	22	15
Competitor #3	12	14	11	7

Figure 34

Figure 35 shows the features that are most important to each customer group and the percentage of the market attributable to each group. (Each customer group is in essence an industry.) Sales by the "company" and by its three competitors total 100%.

Customer group #1: Chemical and oil refineries.
35% of market
Continuous operation places a premium on operating savings. Product feature "A", high resistance to corrosion from chemical vapors reduces maintenance.

Customer group #2: Transportation companies.
30% of market
Reliability and the availability of quality service are important due to the high cost of downtime.

Customer group #3: General industrial plants.
25% of market
Companies are willing to pay for value, but no attribute or feature is uniquely important.

Customer group #4: Government entities.
10% of market
Purchases are based on low price from previously approved vendors.

Figure 35

Conclusions derived from figures 32 through 35.

1. Competitor #3 has been the major supplier to customer group #4 (government entities). It has an uninspiring product, but one that meets minimum requirements.

2. In customer group #1 (chemical & refining) the "company" has a commanding competitive advantage over all three competitors, due to product feature "A" and operating savings.

3. In customer group #2 (transportation) the company has a commanding competitive advantage over competitors #1 & #3, due to reliability and service. It has a slight advantage over competitor #2 due to its product being more reliable. Product feature "D" where competitor 2 could have an advantage is not considered important by the industry.

4. In customer group #3 (general industry) the company has a demonstrably better product than competitors #1 & #4, but no major advantage over competitor #2.

Based on these conclusions the company could take the following actions to increase total income and cash generation.

(A) Establish a separate series of model numbers for the chemical and refining industry (the largest market segment), retaining all existing features and attributes. Establish a premium price for these models, taking care not to overprice. Publish sales literature for this industry that emphasizes the benefits of the product to this industry and establish a justification for the premium price.

(B) Retain the original models, but without corrosion protection, as the basic model. The basic units, without corrosion protection, can remain available for those chemical and refining customers who do not wish to purchase the premium product. Investigate the possibility of cost reducing product feature "B" and placing this feature on a par with competitors.

(C) Organize the service function so that it is focused on the transportation industry. Emphasize reliability in all communications with the transportation industry. With no change in product price the company should be able to take share away from competitors #1 and #4 and improve its competitive posture versus competitor #3. The company also may be able to take advantage of the differentiation in service by raising the prices for service and for spare parts.

(D) Examine the possibility of introducing a low cost line to compete with competitor # 3 in the government (bid) market segment. The cost of participating in this segment probably will outweigh the potential gains, but having a readily available low cost product strategy can provide a defensive position. Reduce costs by scaling back on the sales effort directed at the government segment.

This hypothetical example illustrates product line segmentation (corrosion resistant product), market segmentation (transportation market), alignment of resources to reduce costs (reducing government sales effort) and focus on product strength (service to the transportation industry) while emphasizing the importance of differentiation.

There are literally hundreds of ways to segment a market. The consumer market, for example, can be segmented by age, income, education, geographic location, military service etc. It can be sub-segmented further such as by age then by education. There are ample texts describing this process.

The CEO's task is not only to be certain that marketing has analyzed and segmented the market, but also to assure that the marketing strategy has been based on the correct segmentation.

2. Redefine your distribution channels.

There is a strong possibility that distribution channels for a mature product are not as efficient as they might be. Inefficiencies can be the result of changes in the market and distributor organizations, over time. The first thing to look for are overlapping channels of distribution. The second is to identify whether the most efficient channels are being used. The third is to evaluate whether each distributor or representative is performing up to expectations.

The hierarchy of the different channels is worth examining as are the functions they provide. Channels for an industrial company could include the following.

(a) Company sales force. Dedicated solely to the company's products. Best qualified to sell value or to perform application engineering on technical products. Inventory is carried by the company. Company controls pricing decision to customer.

(b) Manufacturers representatives. Handle several products. Emphasizes those products that are the easiest to sell or provide the greatest return on their efforts. Can sell value and be creative if its worth the effort. Inventory is still carried by the company. Receives a commission even if sale also involves a distributor. Company retains control over pricing decision to customer, but is at risk where a representative uses a portion of his commission for rebates to customers or for buying influence. Representative's commissions should be kept at a reasonable level and be controlled by senior management to protect the company from illegal or unethical practices.

(c) Distributor. Usually in closest geographic proximity to customer. Provides routine sales coverage. Usually stocks inventory making it easier for customer to obtain product, while also reducing the company's own inventory. Salesmen are usually not technically qualified or oriented to selling value. (Distributor salesmen have sometimes been referred to as order takers). Company loses considerable control over pricing decision since product is owned by distributor who is at liberty to use his discount to reduce price to user.

(d) Influence channels. Industry experts, engineering firms, and anyone else to whom the buyer looks to for information or guidance. The buyer views influence channels as objective third parties.

Marketing needs to reevaluate these channels to be certain they are being used effectively and at the lowest cost to the company. Included in the cost is the support required for each channel. It is true, for example, that manufacturer's representatives only get paid when they sell the product. Yet, they need sales literature, product information, training, and company salesmen backing them up. The more technical the product the more likely it will be necessary for company salesmen to call on the customer in support of the manufacturer's representative. Manufacturer's representatives are not, therefore, a completely variable cost.

3. Keep the product from becoming a commodity.

Though the product is mature, marketing must always be looking for ways to differentiate the product from the competition, by seeking new applications or product modifications that will give the company a competitive advantage. The CEO needs to be certain that marketing is fulfilling its role as the company's interface with the market so that new ideas are brought forth. Without exercising some leadership in this regard the company can easily fall behind a competitor who is more responsive to the marketplace. The Japanese have not only introduced products to compete against mature U.S. products, they have been innovative as well. SONY's walkman radio is an excellent example of how a mature commodity product is modified to create an exciting new market niche.

Section Four

Operations

Seven areas for cost improvements.

Cost reduction is one of operations' primary objectives in a mature company. Maintaining high morale and keeping employees attention focused on quality, while reducing costs, is a major challenge.

There are seven broad cost reduction areas to be addressed, each requiring the participation of key groups in the organization.

(1) Direct material costs.

(2) Inventory costs.

(3) Direct labor costs, including benefits.

(4) Indirect wage and salary costs, including benefits.

(5) Indirect material costs.

(6) Systems and procedures costs.

(7) Other indirect costs, such as electricity.

Achieving significant savings in each of these seven areas of opportunity is the classic industrial engineering challenge. Success depends largely on how the various groups within the organization interact, the extent to which they are motivated, and the goals that are established for the cost improvement program. These are the concern of the CEO.

Direct material costs can, for example, be reduced in several ways.

(a) Purchase material at a lower cost.

(b) Change materials to those that are less costly.

(c) Reduce the amount of material used in the design.

Purchasing materials at lower cost (alternative a) is largely the responsibility of a single group, purchasing.

Changing materials (alternative b) will, however, involve several groups. Even a simple material substitution, such as using a different grade of steel, will require an evaluation by engineering and manufacturing engineering. A more complex substitution, such as using powdered metallurgy instead of a machined part, will require an evaluation by engineering and manufacturing engineering plus an accounting analysis to determine whether an investment in new equipment is justified. If the answer is yes, then quality control, purchasing, manufacturing engineering and factory operations become involved in the purchasing, installation and introduction of the new equipment in the factory.

Areas of cost reduction opportunity also overlap. For example, inventory cost reductions can be brought about using "just in time" concepts that require changes to systems and procedures.

The CEO also must know whether his factories are up to date. If the company has been well managed, enjoys cost leadership and has state of the art equipment, systems and processes, the CEO can deal from a position of strength. If, on the other hand, the company does not have cost leadership and the manufacturing operation is out dated, it will be essential to establish priorities.

In either case engineering and manufacturing must be integrated and working toward common goals.

Scrap the traditional cost improvement program.

The traditional approach to organizing cost reduction activities is to establish cost reduction committees (or teams) consisting of representatives from each function (engineering, manufacturing engineering, purchasing, accounting, quality control and shop operations). These committees are structured so that they can cross organization boundaries. A uniform pay back period is usually established for determining whether an improvement is to be implemented. Each committee is assigned a cost improvement budget and each competes with the others to see which committee can achieve the highest over budget variance.

Typically the dollar value of reported cost reductions is staggering. Cost avoidance savings are also typically included with cost reductions. The argument for allowing inflated savings and cost avoidance is that some good is coming from these activities.

The underlying concept behind the traditional cost improvement program is that one idea leads to another. This is frequently depicted as turning over one rock (representing a cost improvement) only to uncover another rock, and so on. Cost improvement committees in the traditionally structured program can accomplish some good.

Install a flexible, task oriented CI program.

The traditional approach, however, lacks the setting of objectives, and this is where the CEO can exert a positive influence.

The objectives themselves will depend on whether the company is the cost leader and has up to date equipment and processes. When the company is the cost leader, time and resources can be allocated to incremental improvements since they will not be quickly made obsolete by major design changes. When the company is not the cost leader it will probably make major design changes or major changes to equipment and processes, that can negate incremental cost improvements. It is counter productive to modify a factory operation if it is going to be made obsolete before the savings can pay back the investment.

The objectives also will depend on the availability of cash for investment in cost improvements. The CEO needs to establish the investment budget, and allocate the portion available to the coat improvement program.

The cost improvement program also represents a commitment of peoples time. Efforts must be focused on activities that have the greatest reward if the company is to succeed.

The steps that need to be taken to establish cost improvement objectives include:

1. Reviewing the design to determine whether there will be a major redesign, and if not, whether specific components will be redesigned to take advantage of lower cost materials or processes.

2. Reviewing shop operations to determine whether major portions of the factory are obsolete, or whether individual equipment or processes are obsolete.

3. Reviewing production and inventory control procedures to determine the extent to which "just in time" inventory practices are in place.

4. Reviewing systems to determine the extent that engineering and factory paperwork have been integrated and eliminated, and the progress made toward the paperless factory.

5. Obtaining information about the equipment and processes used by competitors, comparing them with the company's equipment and processes and then comparing the company's equipment with that which is considered state of the art.

6. Purchase and audit competitive products, to evaluate their cost and quality.

This type of evaluation should be part of the ongoing annual planning cycle and should help establish the operating portion of the company's strategic plan. From this process the CEO and Operations VP can establish guidelines and objectives for the company's cost reduction activity.

Projects, for example, can be organized to address modernizing complete sections of the factory or to redesign product models etc.. These projects, in effect, become cost improvement teams responsible for their assigned areas.

Objectives can then be set for the rest of the cost improvement program. These objectives should be in terms of specific needs, such as:

(a) Reduce the labor content of model xyz by 10%.

(b) Reduce the cost of purchased direct materials by 20%.

(c) Reduce the cost of purchased gasses and electricity by 15%.

One or more cost reduction committee can be assigned responsibility for miscellaneous improvements and for evaluating and implementing employee suggestions.

In addition the CEO can establish criteria for determining whether a cost improvement should be implemented. For example, improvements involving a product model that will be completely redesigned or a factory area that will be modernized, must pay for themselves in less than one year. Cost improvements that relate specifically to other product models must pay for themselves within two years. Cost improvements that relate to consumable gasses and to electrical consumption must pay for themselves in three years. A grid specifying the payback period for different situations can be issued to guide all the cost improvement teams.

The advantages of this approach are that, (a) cost improvement activities are focused on needs, (b) the potential value of the cost improvements can be predetermined, (c) benefits having a short life are required to have a rapid payback while those that are long lasting are permitted a longer payback, and (d) general and spontaneous cost improvements and employee suggestions are not overlooked.

ACTIONS TO CONSIDER TAKING.

1. Keep employees involved.

Regardless of whether quality circles are the best approach for a specific company, the principle of employee involvement should not be overlooked. Participation of the CEO in setting objectives and reviewing progress can help enlist genuine employee support for the cost improvement program.

2. Strengthen the quality program.

One danger that can be easily avoided if addressed by the CEO, is the possibility of reduced quality as the result of cost improvement activities. It is essential for the CEO to establish a firm position that quality will not be sacrificed. If employees have any idea that the CEO is willing to sacrifice quality to achieve savings, the company's entire quality program will suffer. Beech-Nut's recent experience with the purity of its apple juice is a good example of why it is important to avoid even the appearance of sacrificing quality for the sake of cost savings.

3. Invest in flexible manufacturing.

With the advent of computers and microprocessor controls it is now possible to have flexible equipment and processes that reduce set up time, allow shorter production runs and make design changes easier. Long production runs and the stocking of parts was caused largely by the cost of setting up equipment prior to each new run.

An example is the metal tanks (or cans) for distribution transformers, in which the electrical components are mounted with insulating oil. Before inserting the core and coil into the tank for vacuum drying, the core and coil assembly is baked to remove moisture. Different sizes and models of core and coil assemblies can be loaded into the baking oven in any random sequence. When the core and coil comes out of the oven the correct tank must be waiting for it. The core and coil must be immediately inserted into its tank, covered with oil and put into the vacuum process.

The tanks vary in size from one foot to three feet in diameter, and from two feet to five feet in height. Individually they take up a great deal of space. The production line for making tanks was sequential with a fixed conveyor between work stations. The set up time required for each model varied from between 30 minutes to an hour. This inflexible process required that tanks be made in large batches ahead of time. They had to be stored and then located, one at a time, for dispatch to the assembly area to match the core and coil coming out of the drying oven.

A flexible tank manufacturing line would permit tanks to be made one model at a time to match the core and coils. This would eliminate an entire floor of storage area (required to store the inventory of tanks waiting for core and coils), and eliminate the labor required to search for and dispatch the tanks.

Machining centers are also now available to machine fabrications or castings for many different components such as motor frames or engine blocks, where changes in set up can be accomplished at the push of a button. Punch presses, projection or spot welding equipment, and many other operations can be programmed for multiple set ups, changeable at the command of an operator or programmable controller.

Today it is much easier to achieve flexibility in manufacturing. The CEO should make certain that operations is taking advantage of the new technologies that make flexibility possible at a reasonable cost.

Lower set up costs can be the key to affordable flexibility. Lower set up costs permit shorter production runs that result in lower inventory costs and improved customer response time.

4. Be certain technology is up to date.

The CEO should be certain that operations' invests in equipment and processes that, at a minimum, achieve parity with competitors' costs. Preferably each investment should place the company ahead of the competition. The only valid reasons for not investing in the latest technology? Unproven technology, where the risk of investing is great: New equipment or processes with little leverage on total cost: Or the financial payback period is beyond reason.   Unproven new technology should be given a close examination if it can leapfrog the competition in a strategic way. Development of unproven technology should be treated as a research project and brought through the pilot stage before committing the company. It should be viewed as a unique, high risk strategic effort and not a routine investment.

The US steel industry persisted in investing in blast furnaces long after the Japanese and European steelmakers had proven BOF technology and shifted to Basic Oxygen Furnaces. Foreign steelmakers also led the way with continuous casters. Failure to invest in the latest proven technology had as much to do with the lack of competitiveness of the US steel industry as did high wages. Not only were the new blast furnaces (in which US steel companies invested) less productive, but the wrong investment in outdated equipment restricted the availability of cash for new investments and left the US steel companies encumbered with depreciation charges or large write-offs associated with the wrong investment.

The search for up to date processes and equipment should not be confined to the US. Auditing equipment and processes should be an ongoing evaluation of the modernity of the manufacturing activity, with conclusions and actions made an integral part of the company's strategic plan.

5. Keep gamesmanship out of cost improvements.

Everyone must believe in the value of the cost improvement program. It must be viewed as an activity that protects jobs and helps ensure the company's continued success. It cannot be allowed to become just another bureaucratic exercise where gamesmanship is more important than substance.

Inflating savings or rigging cost improvements should have the same stigma attached to them as stealing from a fellow employee. People who cheat on cost improvements or quality are pariahs and should be expurgated from the organization. Wasting resources on inflated cost improvements diminishes the company's ability to compete effectively.

Unfortunately it is easy to rig cost improvements or savings. For example, purchasing can make an initial purchase at a high price knowing that a lower price is available, and then report the next purchase as a cost improvement. Manufacturing engineering can establish a time for an operation knowing that the method will be quickly changed and then report the change as a cost saving. The intention of Cost avoidance reports is to prevent these types of activities by preempting the perceived need to rig savings. Cost avoidance is a legitimate effort and is part of every persons job. Cost avoidance in a cost improvement program is likely to compromise the integrity of the program. The CEO must find a way for both activities to stand on their own.

Task oriented cost improvement committees with specific objectives can help to remove gamesmanship from the program. Leadership is required to assure that everyone views cost improvements as critical and essential.

Section Five

People

People challenges in a mature business.

Attracting good people and motivating longer service (frequently older) employees, are the primary people challenges in a mature company.

Young college graduates are looking for jobs that provide experience and genuine responsibility, with opportunities for advancement. Responsible jobs for new employees and opportunities for advancement are hard to come by in a company that isn't growing. Longer service employees hold the better jobs, have a sense of entitlement and can view change as a threat.

Yet change is what the CEO is striving to achieve; change to rejuvenate existing product lines, to add new products, and to reduce costs while improving quality.

Most actions taken to achieve these changes work against attracting good people and motivating employees. Restructuring and cost improvements will reduce the number of jobs and eliminate opportunities, while aggravating the concerns of longer service employees.

Typically the solution is to provide early retirement for longer service higher level employees, which reduces costs and clears the way for younger employees and new additions. This is an admission of failure, since it confirms that the company allowed the organization to become overstaffed and doesn't have the resources to resolve the issue in a constructive way.

The extent that the CEO can restructure the organization (to achieve the needed savings and improvements in efficiency) and retain longer service employees to work on needed cost improvement or marketing projects, the better the morale and motivation of all employees.

With respect to entry level positions other than direct labor, the CEO should determine whether the company can offer the kinds of responsibilities and opportunities younger people expect. If not, the company is better off not recruiting college graduates over the near term. Eventually it will be necessary to infuse new people into the company. In the near term, good people hired into this environment will feel shortchanged and quickly leave. This is an expensive, disruptive process that hurts morale.

The exception will be where new skills are required. The new skills that are most likely to be needed will be in the areas of programming and communications technologies. If the company has been implementing new technology on a steady basis a cadre of people with these skills will be in place and new recruits can identify with them. When the company starts from a base of older technologies, people with these skills have an opportunity to make a major contribution to the company. Their success in this assignment can be used by them to advance their careers within the company or elsewhere. People with these skills have considerable mobility, and this can be an advantage when a company is trying to catch up. Being certain who to hire is another problem. Programming skills are frequently tied to equipment types or programming languages. Unless the company's needs are clearly identified as to programming language, equipment type or communications technology, it will be difficult to assure that there is a fit between the company and the skills of the prospective employee.

Using temporary employees or hiring a specialty firm such as EDS may help to bridge the gap between traditional and new technologies.

ACTIONS TO CONSIDER TAKING.

1. Obtain employee support for the tough decisions.

The CEO's ability to lead can help obtain the support of all employees in achieving the company's marketing and cost improvement objectives. Communications should explain the need for the company's actions even when the actions are not pleasant. In a smaller company the CEO can interact directly with most employees to explain the reasons for his program and obtain feedback. In larger company's, round table meetings with small groups of employees, coupled with random direct contact in offices and on the factory floor, can help provide feedback.

An open communications program is more likely to succeed if it is merely a continuation of an established and respected program.

2. Reexamine the data processing organization.

Data processing is usually organized within the accounting function and is oriented toward central processing using mainframe or mini computers. It also is usually focused on book-keeping tasks.

Manufacturing and service businesses usually rely on distributed processing, using microprocessor technology closely akin to personal computers.

The CEO needs to assure himself that his organization meets three criteria.

> (1) That the skills required for distributed processing (which is heavily oriented toward communications technology as compared with centralized computer processing) are available and <u>responsible to</u> operations.

(2) That a basic plan is established for integrating all islands of processing with the central computer system.

(3) That responsibility for assuring compliance with (or modifications to) the plan is assigned to a single person.

RISK ANALYSIS

An entrepreneurs' success as CEO will depend heavily on his ability to realistically evaluate risk. Risk has two dimensions. Both dimensions should be considered when making a decision.

The first dimension is probability. The second is the negative consequence of taking or not taking a particular action.

Probability refers to the statistical chance that an event will occur. Negative consequence refers to the potential negative impact of an action on the company.

This simple approach to risk analysis can help the CEO avoid actions that can cripple his company. For example:

1. Protecting the company's financial records.

The issue is whether to incur the expense of maintaining copies of financial records in a remote location where they are protected from fire or natural disaster.

The probability of a fire or natural disaster destroying the company's records may be very small. If the company is located in an area away from hurricanes, tornados or earthquakes the probability of a natural disaster occurring may only be one in five hundred thousand.

Yet the impact on the company of having its financial records destroyed, could be its going out of business.

In this example the probability of disaster is low but the negative consequences are catastrophic. Not protecting the company's financial records is a high risk decision.

2. Repairing a 100KVA electric transformer.

In this situation a service company that routinely repairs electrical equipment is asked to quote on repairing a small transformer at a farm. There is a standby transformer that can be used while the damaged unit is being repaired. The issue is whether to quote the job.

The probability of the transformer failing after it has been repaired is low, perhaps one chance in a hundred thousand.

The impact on the company if the transformer fails is the cost of removing, repairing the transformer a second time and reinstalling the repaired unit, for a total out of pocket cost of perhaps one thousand dollars.

The combination of low probability of failure and the low negative impact on the company if the transformer does fail, make the decision to quote a low risk decision.

3. Repairing a 100KVA PCB electric transformer.

The same service company used in the above example is asked to quote on the same size transformer by a steel mill. The major difference between the two situations is that the unit at the steel mill is filled with a fire retardant insulating oil containing PCB's. The issue is whether to quote the job.

The probability of the PCB transformer failing after it has been repaired is low, perhaps one chance in a hundred thousand.

The EPA considers PCB's to be a toxic material. If the fire retardant oil containing PCB's is spilled while the transformer is being removed or transported from the steel mill, the service company will be required to clean up the spill of hazardous material. The cost of clean up and consequential damages could be as low as $10,000 or as great as $1,000,000 if people were exposed to the PCB's.

By taking precautions the probability of spilling PCB's is low.

Undertaking the repair of this transformer is a high risk decision. The negative consequences of an accidental spill are potentially enormous, though the probability of a spill are low.

The following table illustrates this approach to risk analysis.

Probability	& Negative Consequence	= Conclusion
Low.	Negligible impact.	Low risk
High.	Negligible impact.	Fairly low risk
Low.	High impact.	High risk.
High.	High impact.	Very high risk.

Defining risk in this manner allows the CEO to evaluate risk versus reward and helps to keep him from assuming unwarranted risks. This should not impede boldness. It merely implies that very high risk actions should be avoided unless the reward truly warrants taking the action.

APPENDIX

NOTES

Part 1, page 22
From Parkinson's Law, by C. Northcote Parkinson.

Part 2, page 74
Learning curve theory was used by corporate purchasing departments when negotiating contract prices following WWII. For information on the original use of learning curves refer to various US government documents.

For additional views on the application of learning curves to business strategies refer to Perspectives on Experience by The Boston Consulting Group.

Part 3, page 119
There are numerous formulas that purport to show the most economic order quantity for purchasing or for the lot size of a production run. The terms used by the formula in Part 3 are defined below.

$$EOQ = (2*C*N/P*I + 2*F*A)^{1/2}$$

EOQ, Economic order quantity.
C, Total cost to prepare purchase order.
N, Number of units consumed in one year.
P, Purchase price of one unit including freight cost.
I, Cost of money in decimal.
F, Floor area (sq ft) required to store one unit.
A, Annual storage charge ($/sq.ft.).

Part 3, page 144

Work sampling has been used for identifying inefficient methods in the factory and office. It has been an effective tool for improving productivity of indirect labor.

Work sampling is the use of probability theory to predict the composition of a population of events, based on a small statistical sample. The events can be observations of people working, or not working. The use of random sampling techniques is well established. Election polls are the most familiar use of this theory.

To be statistically valid the observations must be random and be sufficiently large in number. It should be pointed out that one person or one machine that is observed represents one observation. This means that an observation made on entering an office where fifteen people are seen to be either working or not working, results in fifteen observations for the sample.

PRICING DATA

Assumptions:
Total market size, constant in no growth market = $1 million
Number of companies in highly concentrated market = 5
Number of companies in moderately concentrated market = 10
Number of companies in fragmented market = 40
Income as a percent of sales = 5%
Savings from cost improvement programs as percent of sales = 1%
No dominant company.

Table #1. Three scenarios with no dominant company.

MARKET CONCENTRATION-->	Highly concentrated.		Moderately concentrated.		Fragmented.	
	$	% share	$	% share	$	% share
Total	1,000	100	1,000	100	1,000	100
Company # 1	220	22	120	12	40	4
Company # 2	215	21	108	11	27	3
Company # 3	189	19	97	10	25	3
Company # 4	188	19	97	10	25	3
Company # 5	188	19	97	10	25	3
Company 6.......n	0	0	97	10	25	3

Table 2 shows the sales increases that must be achieved by company #1 under the three scenarios outlined in Table #1, to have total income equal the initial income plus cost savings. It also shows the extent of the increase in market share required to achieve these sales and the average amount of sales lost by each competitor. For the sake of simplicity the 1% price reduction applies only to the increased sales, otherwise the original sales would also decrease by 1%.

Table #2 (Dollars in thousands except % where shown.)

Scenario	Original	Increase	Total	Sales lost by competitors
#1				
Sales	220	44	264	11
Market share %	22%	4%	26%	
Income @ 5%	11	2.2	13.2	
Cost Improvements	2.2			
Income + CI	13.2			
#2				
Sales	120	24	144	2.7
Market share %	12%	2%	14%	
Income @ 5%	6	1.2	7.2	
Cost Improvements	1.2			
Income + CI	7.2			
#3				
Sales	40	8	48	.2
Market share %	4%	1%	5%	
Income @ 5%	2	0.4	2.4	
Cost Improvements	0.4			
Income + CI	2.4			

INDEX